AMAZON FBA

*THE ULTIMATE GUIDE ON
HOW TO MAKE MONEY
ONLINE THROUGH AMAZON
FBA TO EARN PASSIVE
INCOME*

BRUCE BLEVINS

ISBN: 9781078144735

Table of Contents

CONCLUSION

INTRODUCTION

Amazon's FBA program is a fantastic open door for the large group of spectators of business visionaries. Particularly those that are beginning as a one-person shop. What's exceptional with Amazon FBA is its adaptability. As a one-person shop, you can contend with the higher and progressively settled seller. Private ventures are constrained in storage space and the time management to sell, rundown, make, and ship orders. You can satisfy small orders (ex. 20 every day) as well as the bigger orders (ex. 100,000 every day), which interpret that you can begin as a mother and pop shop and thrive as a bigger corporate utilizing Amazon's Fulfillment. You would now be able to deal with the increased volume effectively while managing your stock and spending you to source your product.

This will decrease the upper hand of the more exceptional seller and empower you to make a good pay and develop as large as you want. Consider it. You need access to your product(s) of decision. Amazon FBA gives a surge of pay that you can take to an unheard-of level. At every fulfillment center, (Amazon has more than 65) you are employing at LOW rates per order a staff that deals with the order processing, shipping, and customer.

The seller has to source your product(s), invest your energy processing those things, and shipping them to Amazon. A portion of the critical advantages of Amazon FBA

- You approach tens of millions of Prime customers

Scale order taking care of and construct coordination both on and off Amazon·

- Sell all around by utilizing the FBA export program to access customers all-inclusive at no extra expense to you.
- Multi-Channel Fulfillment (MCF) is a discretionary program by FBA that enables you to easily use Amazon's reality class Fulfillment Centers for your off-Amazon orders.

- What's more, take a paid get-away while FBA works for you satisfying customer orders and managing customer service.

- You approach tens of millions of Prime customers

- FBA now speaks to a growing 45% of Amazon's revenues
- Amazon Prime began in 2005
- In 2009 Prime had 2 million members; in 2011 there were more than 5 million; in 2014 there are more than 20 million members
- Prime speaks to just 6% of Amazon's absolute customers up until now
- Prime is growing at over 20% Year Over Year
- Prime customers burn through 140% more than regular Amazon Customers
- 40 % - 50 % of Amazon customers have never purchased from an outsider

With FBA, Amazon can help improve your online deals and keep customers cheerful, while sparing you sufficient time so you can concentrate on growing your business

CHAPTER ONE

Introduction to Fulfilment by Amazon!

Simple access, great decision, and quick processing are not many of the unbounded charms of e-commerce. At the point when abused shrewdly, these components can be similarly useful both for purchasers and sellers. To draw in purchasers and appreciate huge sales income, online brokers need to satisfy broadly foreseen requirements of e-commerce. Meeting all market demands and remaining concentrated on every single detail of your business can be boisterous for any e-trader. At such occasions, you have to procure additional assistance to arrange your regular business and to direct the entirety of its tasks easily. Fulfillment by Amazon is one such ingenious web service, which gives some assistance to vendors by expertly playing out the problematic and touchy order fulfillment process for their sake.

Fulfillment by Amazon (FBA) is a beneficial program intended to furnish sellers with the storeroom for their inventory and execute orders from Amazon fulfillment center. In any line of e-commerce, prepared capacity and unfaltering fulfillment are fundamentally important for by and large business development, customer fulfillment, and benefit augmentation. FBA presents people and little endeavors just as huge partnerships with the chance to surpass the desires for their customers with protected, brilliant, and fast order conveyance. Presently, if you are a maker or a wholesaler, you can give all out consideration to your buying and production as by profiting FBA you are never again required to keep up your distribution center and endure overwhelming placement cost. You don't need to stress over product pressing and shipment regardless of size or frequency of the orders.

The arrangement of Fulfillment by Amazon may sound confused; however, by and by, it's easy to pursue as it is extensively made remembering precise trading demands and most recent e-commerce patterns. When you have sent your fresh out of the plastic new or utilized products to the fulfillment center, they are kept in Amazon storehouses in prepared to ship shape. Amazon starts order fulfillment for your products after getting orders from customers through its website or upon your direct solicitation for their shipment. This system is trailed by elevating off the predefined things from inventory to hence pressing them for dispatch. At long last, the ordered products are sent from Amazon fulfillment centers to the said goals. After the derivation of fulfillment charges, net sale sum is credited to your record, and the same process is rehashed for next exchanges. You can be guaranteed that every one of the means included is performed consequently flawlessly in an expert way by the most trusted, productive, and experienced hands of Amazon.

It is anyway important to take note of that stocks under FBA dependably stay under seller's possession and control. As there are no upper or lower inventory limits, you can include or pull back your products from fulfillment stores at whatever point you like. Likewise, order frequency isn't necessary at all since fulfillment charges are deducted at the purpose of sale. A portion of the other incredible highlights of FBA incorporate redid order processing, protection, and robotized following. At last, it tends to presume that Fulfillment by Amazon underlines that you should focus on your production, sales, and the executives without being stressed a dime over order fulfillment.

A Quick Explanation

What is Amazon FBA?

As an entrepreneur or person who is hoping to sell products through Amazon, having the opportunity to exploit Fulfillment by Amazon can be very advantageous. With the capacity to limit the amount of time that you would spend selling and delivering your products, Fulfillment by Amazon does a large portion of the work for you. If you're as of now keen on these services, underneath is data and how it very well may be helpful for your selling needs.

The Fulfillment Process

The whole procedure is generally straightforward. You will be allowed to store your products in one of Amazon's fulfillment focuses. When a customer purchases something that you have available to be bought, they will pick, pack, and ship it for you. Additionally, customer service will distribute to every product that you are hoping to sell. That implies that if your purchaser has any questions, customer service will deal with the issues.

Fees

Another considerable advantage related to utilizing Amazon FBA is that you will almost certainly exploit their services for a negligible cost. As a savvier arrangement than opening your very own warehouse and pressing/transporting your goods, you can take out this tedious errand without paying absurd fees. You will most likely spend as you go when you begin working with Amazon. Each organization will be charged by the space that you use in the warehouse and the number of requests that Amazon satisfies.

What to Sell Using Amazon FBA

One of the most significant advantages related to utilizing Amazon's Fulfillment to sell your goods is that many different categories told you what to sell. Most of the sellers list their products in the "Open Categories" area because of the way that posting products under these categories do not require approval. A portion of the Open Categories accessible to organizations include:

- Amazon Kindle
- Books
- Baby Products
- Cameras and Photos
- Cell Phones
- Home and Garden
- Accessories for Electronics

Different categories accessible for individuals pondering what to sell utilizing Amazon FBA are known as "Proficient Seller Categories." To list your products here, you will require approval. A portion of these categories include:

- Automotive and Power sports
- Beauty
- Collectible Coins
- Clothing and Accessories
- Fine Art
- Gift Cards
- Grocery and Gourmet Food

These are only a couple of supportive tips and indications to help you as you push ahead with your fulfillment business.

What Is Amazon FBA?

An inquiry that is on numerous people's lips is "What Is Amazon FBA"? To enable me to clarify what Amazon FBA is, let us take a gander at a little story, of how Amazon FBA can allow you to take your internet offering business to the following level.

Amazon FBA or to give it, it's full name Fulfillment by Amazon is a program set up by Amazon that enables you to use Amazon to a warehouse and afterward send out your items (and furthermore dependably you to sell your items on the Amazon Site). Amazon FBA is straightforward and yet is exceptionally incredible and can take your business to the following level for little costs.

Envision the scene you are caught up with doing your product sourcing and have picked up individual books, CD's DVD's, Home and Beauty items a couple of new toys (Yes items sold through Amazon FBA must be either new or collectible). Presently ordinarily at the back of your mind, you suppose I wish I could purchase increasingly stock, however, there is no more space at home. This is the place the Amazon FBA becomes possibly an essential factor. Also, you can try things out of utilizing the essential Amazon selling record, or you can be a Pro-Merchant, it doesn't make a difference.

You get back home and output or rundown the items as regular into your Amazon selling account and a couple of clicks later, you print out some bar codes which you should put over the first bar code on the item (Yes items should have a bar code or recorded on the Amazon site). A couple of more clicks and you print out a pressing slip which goes in the box or boxes. You at that point book a get from the transporter, and this depends on where you live and how you pay for it - every nation is extraordinary.

Next, you complete the order and trust that the order will be picked up and inside days your item will be in the Amazon warehouse being sold for you, and you can kick back and bank the money. Amazon FBA deals with installments, transportation, and customer emails. You need to source progressively stock and bank the money.

Indeed, there are some additional costs that Amazon charges yet these are low, and the investment funds you make on the postage is awesome - recall you are utilizing Amazon's purchasing power and no more lines in Post Offices and no all the more purchasing air pocket wrap and boxes.

Something different people don't understand is that you can use Amazon FBA to ship out to your eBay and various purchasers. Indeed, Amazon store the items, and send the items out for you. Furthermore, for next to no cost and much of the time significantly less expensive than you can do. All the pricing information can be found on your countries Amazon site. Complete a quest for Amazon FBA.

Go on and give it a go, you don't have anything to lose and a ton to pick up.

Amazon FBA Tutorial

Amazon "FBA" (Fulfillment by Amazon) is an administration offered by Amazon, whereby you can stock your products in Amazon's warehouse network.

The reason you'd need to do this is overwhelming because of the way wherein you're ready to make a lot of money by being related with Amazon - having their group of spectators and social clout behind your image.

While you don't need to be a piece of the FBA program to sell products on the Amazon platform, it's been recognized as the most proficient and adaptable way to accomplish benefit through an advanced business which needn't bother with a gigantic measure of overhead to begin.

The most effective method to "Profit" With It

The specialty of making money comes down to a straightforward procedure - earn more than you spend. This is as valid for business for what it's worth in the "individual" domain.

The issue for a great many people is they end up spending more than they earn, or end up with a wide range of different topics which degrades their center, however, ends up depleting their resources.

Without a doubt, one of the most severe issues confronting entrepreneurs has been what's known as "obstruction to section" - which is essentially how much resources are required to exploit a chance.

For instance, to make viable programming, you generally need in any event ten years of detailed knowledge, with a specific mastery creating out of it.

Over this, you likewise need market demand and the capacity to give a significant product paying little mind to the different market conditions existing at the time.

Amazon - and retail when all is said in done - needs none of this. You need a product which satisfies market demand, enabling clients to discover it and buy as required. While you could do this with your very own internet business outlet, the heaviness of Amazon's image and its related trust is by a wide margin increasingly significant in verifying the powerful methods by which you're ready to pull in genuine purchasers.

Is FBA Necessary?

At last, FBA is just a "technique" through which you're ready to stock products on Amazon and have them deal with all the conveyance.

A great many people don't need to utilize the "FBA" course; they can sell their products and ship them from their home/office. You can, in any case, do this without really sending bundles to Amazon to send out for your benefit.

What Is the Amazon FBA Program All About?

To begin, the Amazon FBA program represents Fulfillment by Amazon. This is a service Amazon provides to permit online and disconnected sellers to send their goods to Amazon, and Amazon will pack and dispatch the products to singular clients for your sake. You may not know how large the Amazon commercial center is if you don't visit there regularly. They have made some fantastic progress from merely selling books, to now selling pretty much anything.

You can likewise sell products on Amazon and not utilize their FBA service, so you deliver your products, yet there are many preferences of using the FBA system, which will save your time and provide a progressively robotized business arrangement.

It is hugely a comparable service that other drop shippers provide. However, Amazon holds your goods in one of their satisfaction focuses. The service will send your products anytime and to anyplace for your sake. This system can be additionally incorporated with your website to create a completely mechanized system for sending Amazon your goods, and for Amazon shipping them to clients. The expenses for the service are incredibly aggressive, and you pay for real stockpiling and shipments, at discount Amazon rates, they don't charge a charge to utilize the system.

So, for what reason would it be advisable for you to think about utilizing Amazon's system?

Here is a portion of the key focuses of the FBA system:

- You can sell nearly anything on Amazon, or through your very own website and have them pack and send.
- By computerizing your website with Amazon, it implies the business can keep running on autopilot, and you can remove time if you pick, and your business still capacities.
- Send all your stock to Amazon, and they will deal with everything, you should gather your benefits.
- Amazon is currently outranking eBay on Alexa for traffic, and they are a noteworthy contender to eBay.
- Some eBay sellers are utilizing the Amazon FBA to transport goods sold through eBay.

To figure out how to begin using this system, and to create online pay streams, you can get read about it on http://www.Amazon.com. They provide all the essential data on the beginning. You can sell anything as I expressed previously. For instance, just as books, Amazon has classifications like eBay, which spread pretty much anything you can consider for the home, garden, office, dress, sports, etc.

Given the FBA program, and the massive traffic that Amazon generates, you could create an Amazon website, discover products to sell and be ready for action with an online business in all respects rapidly with the instruments they provide. It is presumably one of the least demanding approaches to start an online business right now.

Simple Start with Amazon FBA!

Amazon made something many refer to as Fulfillment by Amazon, which works a lot like eBay, yet as I would like to think, is MUCH better.

For some time, eBay was the first spot to sell things on the web. eBay is extraordinary, yet it requires a lot of work on your part: sourcing, posting, shipping, customer support, and so forth.

If you plan to offer to on the web, at that point, you ought to firmly consider Amazon's fulfillment program called FBA. FBA means "Fulfillment by Amazon," which makes it a fulfillment company. A fulfillment company gives stockpiling and shipping services to its customers' products. FBA is one of a kind because Amazon is likewise the commercial center for those items, so they have a functioning enthusiasm for seeing the items sell. What makes FBA much increasingly phenomenal is that its details are likewise qualified for Amazon's shipping advancements including Free Super Saver Shipping and

Amazon Prime.

It is critical to see how FBA works and how different organizations are utilizing FBA.

Amazon buyers use Prime, so they get free shipping. They effectively spend more on things like flavors, espresso, tea, socks, toilet paper, towels, cleanser, and so on. They contribute significantly more because they completely TRUST Amazon. This is useful for sellers because it implies that you will make more and sell more.

Amazon is an ace of internet commerce and has set the bar exceptionally high for its customers, sellers, and proprietors. Customer service is necessary for them, and we are taking advantage of this utilizing Fulfillment by Amazon. You, as the product seller, never again need to manage the customer service after the deal. You continue sending more products to Amazon, and they deal with the rest.

This book will cover just setting up your Amazon account for FBA. We will go more into sending your products to Amazon, putting away and shipping your products at Amazon, and dealing with your FBA inventory in up and coming articles.

1. Open an Amazon Account

If you have never acquired nor sold on Amazon and

don't have an account, go to the Amazon website and snap on the Selling on Amazon link at the base of any page.

2. Set Up our Amazon Account

When you have an Amazon selling account, contact the Amazon customer service office to set up your account for FBA. Having a good FBA rep on your account will assist you with any issues later on. The rep will walk you through your first shipment.

CHAPTER TWO

FBA - Fulfillment by Amazon

You may have found out about FBA on numerous websites, particularly on Amazon. FBA represents Fulfillment by Amazon. What is it, and how can it work? Would you be able to set aside cash or appreciate different benefits with this offer or process? If you are searching for answers to these inquiries, you are on the right page.

FBA is a process through which Amazon keeps a stock of a seller's goods and afterward show them on their site available to be purchased. Besides this, the organization gets installments for each order set on the web, and the conveys the expected goods to every buyer.

With the assistance of this process, a ton of stores has delighted in a good deal of development in their sales. A few stores have Amazon complete the orders for goods. Ordinarily, the products are sent straightforwardly to the buyers by the sellers selling legitimately on Amazon. Now and again, it occurs by the sellers on different websites, for example, Etsy, eBay that transition to the FBA. Along these lines, it's fascinating to know how this offer by the large store has benefited individuals everywhere throughout the world.

As per numerous sellers, they have encountered a noteworthy ascent in their sales volume. Then again, buyers accept that they are buying from a commendable trust organization rather than a person. Purchasing straightforwardly using FBA adds to the trust of the buyer in the provider. In this way, they may purchase again not far off.

Besides this, sellers can make use of this offer to accomplish numerous different benefits. If you use this administration as a seller, you won't need to worry about the advancement of the product. Also, it will be Amazon's duty to deal with buyers and satisfy orders. Then again, you can concentrate on different tasks, for example, getting new products and do various tasks that may make your business much higher.

Extra benefits:

If you are a product owner, you can take some vacation days without worrying about who will deal with your business while you are away. Your business will continue running while you are having an extraordinary time with your companions in Paris. Thus, you can avoid your office for the same number of days as you need. For whatever length of time that Amazon has your products in their stock, you are a great idea to go, and you don't have to worry about anything.

A few people don't prefer to deal with buyers legitimately. They think that it is hard to deal with troublesome clients. Dealing with pressure isn't some tea. Amazon will handle these things.

If you know nothing about FBA yet, realize that figuring out how to use it isn't hard in any way. You can go to the official website of Amazon to download the pdf documents to find out about how to begin. Inside a couple of minutes, you will be acquainted with the entire framework.

Along these lines, if you have your very own store, you can benefit from this incredible administration offered by Amazon.

How Amazon FBA Helps Entrepreneurs

Amazon FBA is an excellent method to ensure that you can have your products sold and delivered straightforwardly to customers with the goal that you don't need to stress over the shipping and handling procedure. It can likewise be beneficial for organizations who are unfit to have a sufficient measure of storage space for their merchandise, as they house your products on location. So, Fulfillment by Amazon is essentially the ideal part for each seller. Preceding joining, it is prompted that you ensure that it is the right offer for you by deciding how your products achieve your customers, how you can have control of the procedure and the scalability of the program.

How Your Products Reach Amazon Prime Customers?

The main segment to think about when selling with Fulfillment by Amazon is the way your products will achieve Amazon Prime customers. When you use Amazon FBA, the majority of your customers that have an Amazon Prime record will be given a chance to choose two-day shipping for nothing. Nearby Prime customers, ordinary Amazon customers will almost certainly exploit the free shipping with requests of $35.00 or more. One of the most significant advantages related to posting with FBA is that your products will be recorded without a shipping cost for Amazon Prime customers, enabling you to expand your deals.

What is Amazon FBA Seller Central?

Amazon FBA Seller Central is the part of the Amazon site that you will most likely use to have full command over what warehouse your items will be loaded, by the way, you need to list your items, and how you will show the selling highlights of your products. It is essentially a whole dashboard committed to your products and how they will be seen by general society. You will most likely quest for your products once they have been included, take a gander at different costs of contending FBA sellers, and figure out what steps you need Amazon to take during the deal, for example, shipping the products. Seller Central is necessary to the selling procedure as it will give the "early introduction" that your customers get when they discover your products.

What is the Scalability of Amazon FBA?

Amazon FBA scalability is another significant factor to think about when working with Amazon. As your business develops, you will need to ensure that Amazon will grow with you to ensure that each request is satisfied adequately. With scalability offered by the program, you can rest guaranteed that Amazon will most likely help you during peak seasons and provide more assets when you are selling more products. With the capacity to pack and ship either a single unit or a great many various units, the choices are perpetual.

How to Use the Amazon FBA Platform for Your Multichannel Orders?

Amazon.com is the biggest online commercial center, and the platform continues developing. It offers astonishing conceivable outcomes for online retail businesses to showcase products to innumerable customers. If you are selling on Amazon.com, you are unquestionably going an ideal way. Be that as it may, if you are just offering on Amazon, you might miss out on more product sales. It may seem like a provoking errand to expand to more systems, yet since you are as of now selling on Amazon.com, it will be anything but difficult to use different platforms to boost your sales like the Amazon FBA platform.

Amazon.com gives a Multiple Channel Fulfillment (MCF) choice that will enable you to grow to more sales platforms with scarcely any additional costs.

What Is Amazon Multi-Channel Fulfillment?

The FBA support from Amazon meets your Amazon orders, as the MCF decision satisfies buys from every single other system. You can assign most fulfillment to Amazon. Regardless of whether you sell items up for sale sites, Shopify, any other platform, Amazon will pick and channel products to your clients. You essentially need to pay for transportation and dealing with.

Multi Funnel Fulfillment empowers you to pick standard, two-day, or 24-hour delivery, and it computes transportation and delivery costs relying upon the size of the item combined with the selected dispatching approach.

If you might want to use Amazon.com MCF, there are a couple of necessities you have to consider. To begin with, you must be approved for FBA, and that implies you have charge cards on record with Amazon. Those cards will be charged for fulfillment costs, except if your seller account has a positive equalization after that MCF expenses will be subtracted from your dependability.

You ought to likewise have an expert seller account with Amazon to use MCF which as a rule costs $39. 99 every month, be that as it may, you don't pay for product list charges.

Exploit Amazon's MCF with These rules Amazon's MCF is a brilliant procedure for online stores insofar as you use FBA and may adhere to the previously mentioned necessities. In any case, there are a few things that may make this better still for you just as your customers.

Make use of Messaging on Packing Slips.

With Amazon MCF, logos and customization are constrained. You can't comprise of customized embeds or pressing slides. You could have specific communications imprinted on the bundling slide. Make a large portion of these different messages to display that you esteem the client's business and worth them as customers.

Change Prices Depending on the Platform

One useful thing concerning multichannel selling is that you could plan costs to boost your income. For example, if you are offering a product on Amazon, it may require a minimal effort to be competitive. That similar product on another system that isn't as competitive thus can cost more.

Set Aside Some Profits

This tip makes business sense any place you sell products on the web. You never can tell when eccentric costs can come up. With MCF, notwithstanding, the estimating can be cost-successful, you may need to pay for things like delivery and overseeing supplies, and account costs. Regardless of whether you do pass these costs on to clients, it is typically a smart thought to have some cash set aside for if you have an unusual item and need to list it to other product sales channels rapidly.

Retail Arbitrage and Drop Shipping: The Way of Amazon FBA

Why It Works with Amazon FBA Drop Shipping

The standards of buy low/sell high are especially in actuality on the web! You can without much of a stretch join the race to make cash online by applying the exceptionally straightforward standards of buy low/sell high! Satisfaction by Amazon has made creating a social benefit on everyday items that you buy a genuine plausibility locally.

Retail arbitrage is not another thought, yet it has taken on another significance utilizing the web as your market place. You can without much of a stretch buy items locally at deep discounts from discount chains/drugstores and resell them for a benefit utilizing Amazon FBA drop shipping.

Retail arbitrage is an incredible method to make some cash without making remarkable strides. Consider it along these lines if you exploit a provincial just type sale that implies you are getting it that individuals the nation over or on the opposite side of the world don't approach. Your investment funds can transform into your cash cow!

Categories of Items to Sell Using Retail Arbitrage

The conceivable outcomes are very boundless when you consider it. You can resell everything from sustenance to undergarments. To see achievement, you need to know the market for retail items and tap into that market. The categories of items to sell utilizing retail arbitrage are just about all that you would buy in a typical physical building.

You can even sell used items on Amazon! There are a few items that are disallowed available to be purchased on Amazon. Things like hazardous items and other confined items. More data is accessible at the Amazon site.

Utilizing Amazon FBA

When you begin using Amazon FBA to sell your items, you will effectively comprehend why it works with FBA shipping. The procedure is easy to start. You register to pay a little charge as a seller. Choose which items you are going to use Amazon, and you make one shipment to Amazon.

You don't need to discover the buyers because Amazon is known comprehensively and has more than 100 million guests on some random day. You likewise don't need to stress over transportation every sale independently. Amazon does it just for you. You don't need to do considerably more than register, pay the charge and ship your items.

A little starting venture of a few hundred dollars to buy your stock AND to join FBA can pay off truly well.

Essential Tips on How to Make Money Online Selling on Amazon

Since its initiation, Amazon has given a stage to individuals, little organizations, and retailers to sell their products and make a fair salary. Anyway, a few people don't have the foggiest idea of how to make money selling on Amazon. A portion of the means you can follow to turn into a first-class seller in Amazon are recorded beneath.

Follow Amazon selling rules and rules.

In the wake of agreeing to accept a seller account. It is essential to follow all Amazon rules and product rules to abstain from getting prohibited. This rule can be found in the assistance segment of the Amazon site.

Endeavor to be an Amazon featured merchant

Getting the opportunity to be an Amazon feature merchant is one way of explaining the question of how to make money selling on Amazon. Although Amazon does not say the particular recipe on how one turns into a featured merchant, one can without much of a stretch join this renowned gathering following a couple of months by having great deals and astounding customer feedback.

Be adaptable on your estimating

Although everybody's primary point is to make the most extreme profits, it is essential to have a viable valuing procedure. Check the prices of your rivals and ensure the price difference margin is reasonable. In the event your product gets more orders, you can somewhat build the price to boost profits.

Comprehend Amazon expenses and fees

The most effective way on the best way to make money selling on Amazon is understanding the fees and costs included. When you purchase a product to sell on Amazon, you need to price it such that you will take care of your expense and still make a conventional profit.

You can wipe out delivery fees by utilizing Fulfillment by Amazon, FBA, which involves sending your products to Amazon who will at that point handle the bundling and transporting to customers. Amazon likewise charges an assortment of fees, including selling and referral fees.

Exploit Amazon marketing tools

Amazon has a few marketing tools that can enable your products to get took note. A portion of these tools incorporates Listmania, Likes, and Tags.

Ensure you have enough products to satisfy the market need

Although most sellers begin little, it is fitting to have enough product supply in the event you start getting more orders. This ensures your customers don't search for choices and you increment your salary.

Use Amazon seller focal.

An ideal way on the best way to make money selling on Amazon is always to use the seller focal reports. These reports encourage one break down sells potential customers and the adequacy of advancement and marketing.

CHAPTER THREE

3 Ways to Sell Physical Products Using Fulfillment by Amazon (FBA)

Did you realize that Amazon isn't the seller of everything on Amazon? Did you recognize that standard people like you and me can sell physical products on Amazon? This open door has been around for some time, yet it is ending up exceptionally prominent right now because of instructive courses that are springing up all over.

There are three ways to sell physical products on Amazon:

One is to sell other people's products on Amazon and ship the orders by yourself. Another one is to sell other people's products on Amazon and let Amazon ship and sell your products on Amazon and let Amazon ship them. The first way is called vendor satisfied. You list your product on Amazon's site. However, you fill or ship the orders yourself. The last two methods are called FBA.

Dealer satisfied might be the most straightforward way and least expensive to begin. However, it is much more work. You list your products on Amazon's site. At the point when the products are gotten, you are in charge of really shipping the products to the buyer. And you can even sell things that you have around the house utilizing this technique!

You can likewise utilize FBA to sell other people's products. For this situation, you go to the store and find things that are now selling on Amazon, buy them, put your very own particular UPC label on the product, pack it, create the listing, ship it to the Amazon warehouse and hang tight for the buyer. There are PDA apps that you can use to scan products before you get them to enable you to decide whether you can make a benefit. If you like to shop, are great at finding deals and can ship a crate, at that point this might be the business for you. The other extraordinary thing about utilizing FBA is that your products are qualified for the Amazon Prime program. People who take an interest in this can get free 2-day shipping. Numerous people are eager to pay somewhat more for a product for this comfort.

The second way to utilize the FBA program is to sell your products. You find a product that you can sell, find a private label manufacturer, create your image, and sell your product. This is the most rewarding of the ways to sell on Amazon; notwithstanding, it requires increasingly capital in advance. Likewise, it is progressively unsafe because you need to order inventory.

As should be obvious selling on Amazon is unquestionably something that you can do to acquire additional income or become your full-time business. If you are hoping to begin an online business or you need to add an extra income stream to your current online business, then you should consider FBA.

Moneymaking in Amazon

There are numerous pleasantries that Amazon brings to the table for purchasers and merchants alike. Be that as it may, the ideal way to profit by the online retail website Amazon.com is through being a member and by knowing the various ways you can make cash out of Amazon.

The first and most evident reason is that you have the products and they can enable you to sell it on Amazon itself. Be that as it may, imagine a scenario where you have your website. At that point, you also can have that head begin with your e-business by utilizing Amazon's 1-Click Ordering.

Likewise, through Amazon's product promotions, an expense for each click program that features your products to a large number of online customers, it's as straightforward as transferring your products and putting their cost and voila! It's for the world to see! This program requires insignificant expenses, enables you to acquire traffic on your site, and builds your odds of higher income, with more hits and clicks.

If your business is more service-arranged than that of your products, there is likewise the element of Clickriver Ads, a site which additionally offers the collaborate of your services being advanced nearby your products.

Another way to have the option to boost profiting in Amazon is, however, its Fulfillment by Amazon (FBA) program. Through this, you get the chance to store your products on Amazon's fulfillment focuses, and they can securely and legitimately pack and ship those products, and offer quality customer service, on your sake.

As a dealer, no other site can ensure the exactness of your payments however through Checkout by Amazon, Amazon Simple Pay, and Amazon Flexible Payments, these programs guarantee and have demonstrated extortion recognition and enable your customers to have the option to get to the most secure and confided in online payment arrangements.

Amazon has such a vast amount to offer for everybody of various foundations whether you are a creator, you can likewise profit of CreateSpace, a member of the Amazon gathering of organizations, that gives a quick, simple and conservative way to independently publish and impart your substance to potential customers on Amazon.com and different sites.

As an engineer, you can build your site's productivity by the various programs that are offered, for example, Amazon website, Marketplace Web Services, Fulfillment Web Services, Amazon Web Services, Advertising Web Services (Product Advertising API), Amazon Flexible Payments and Mechanical Turk.

All these member programs, are in a singular exertion of making your online business more state-of-the-art, and customer neighborly, and enable engineers to make more up to date and increasingly inventive ways of taking care of the market, at the click of a catch. They incorporate every one of the apparatuses expected to spruce up your site, up to the ways where payment can be made simpler and increasingly available.

How to Make $10,000+ Per Month with Amazon FBA

Amazon FBA (Fulfillment By Amazon) is a business opportunity given by Amazon to urge business-proprietors to list their products in its marketplace.

The model works by Amazon furnishing clients with the

ability to send their products to its distribution center and having them "satisfied" by the hold mammoth (it sends them out) upon fruitful buy.

The motivation behind why Amazon would do this is partly to get free specialty products which are both unique and significant (you claim the products - they deliver them for you), and slightly to make utilization of their large foundation (which they would pay for anyway).

It additionally adds to their offering as a business, as it gives them a significantly increasingly various cluster of products to add to their portfolio (which is essentially their center upper hand).

The significant, exciting point about the "FBA" model is that it is characteristic of the new "digital" business culture that appears to have turned out to be much progressively predominant after the 2008 accident. Instead of keeping a lot of stock, overheads and considerable group organizations have taken to the Internet and online life to discover purchasers and make lean ventures.

Gone are the days when wholesalers decided the destiny of products. Presently, new businesses, business visionaries, and regular people can make $10,000+ per month salary streams without owning any land. All the foundation, marketing, and satisfaction are dealt with by a free company (Amazon) - to which you take every necessary step of sourcing a fruitful product.

To decide whether you'd like to pick up preferred position from this technique for the venture, I've done this instructional exercise to clarify the process of using Amazon FBA. Instead of attempting to make do with scraps from a neighborhood market, the new "digital" realm with all its guarantee is a standout amongst the ideal ways to get your foot in the entryway of the new universe of big business.

How It Works

All businesses work similarly - purchase/assemble a product, offer the product to a market and any "profit" you're ready to make can either be utilized to live off or reinvest into progressively/better products.

The problem for the vast majority is two-overlap: 1) they have no product 2) they have no access to a market.

Whilst both are genuine problems - which would have been a significant disadvantage in a time without the "digital" medium - times have proceeded onward to the point that boundaries to-section are low to the end that you just genuinely need to have the option to contribute a few $1,000 to have the opportunity of selling to a worldwide group of spectators.

What's more, notwithstanding the way that the "Amazon" opportunity has existed for just about ten years now (anybody can list products in its marketplace), the "FBA" model (which is uninvolved) has just begun to wind up mainstream in the previous two years or somewhere in the vicinity.

If you turned out poorly business school, to quickly disclose how to run an "effective" business, you essentially need to be capable give a product/administration to a large group of spectators. You'd regularly go for around 30% net profit edge (after COGS and promoting costs). How you do this is up to you - the key is to purchase low, sell high.

Presently, because the "digital" realm is enormous doesn't mean it's without how "markets" regularly work. The rivalry is a noteworthy power, similar to the idea that since something is "easy," it tends to be imitated moderately mostly by others (prompting a disintegration of your profits).

Selling on Amazon regularly works by giving access to products which people either don't approach locally, or can get locally yet with significant confinements, (for example, shading/measure issues), or with problems in reliability of supply. While the Amazon marketplace is tremendous - don't figure you can outsmart supply/request.

The genuine trick with "digital" businesses is to give access to unique products (regularly made independent from anyone else or your company) which are just accessible through you. These products must be centered around providing an answer that the vast majority have no clue about, and in this manner makes the suggestion of getting it through the Internet real.

Making a "unique" product is 1,000x quite tricky - the trick with it is to work on answers for your very own problems. Work towards honing a skillset, which you're ready to apply to a more extensive group of spectators, from which you'll have the option to distinguish "products" which can be made and offered as a means to disentangle/tackle problems you've encountered yourself.

To start selling on Amazon, there are a few steps to take:

Sign Up for Amazon Seller Account

The initial step is to get a seller account from Amazon. There are two types of seller account - "individual" and "expert." The individual is free and enables you to list items which as of now exist in the Amazon index. You pay a small fee each time a product is sold. Expert costs $40/month and has no additional "per deal" fees (albeit different prices, for example, a stocking fee and so forth may apply). This is the primary account which enables you to list new items in Amazon's index.

Sign Up for GS1 This enables you to create* scanner tags *. They come in two configurations - UPC (Universal Product Code) and EAN (European Article Number). While these can generally be purchased inexpensively ($10), Amazon, Google, and eBay emphatically suggest utilizing GS1 for institutionalization. By using GS1, you're ready to have your products perceived by any semblance of Amazon. The drawback is the cost. However, it shouldn't generally matter - we always suggest setting aside ~$500 for administrative expenses, of which this would be one.

Make A Legal Company (Optional) If you're hoping to set up a genuine FBA task, you'll need a legitimate business (and ledger). Aside from enabling Amazon to open a business account, it allows you to all the more likely oversee charges (which are famously terrible for putting your own money in a specific limit). This is easy to set up, yet it is just vital if you need to manage Amazon on an FBA premise as it were. If you need to sell products on the system, you're free to do it under your name.

Purchase/Build Boxed Products You at that point, need to get a set of boxed forms of the product. If you make the product yourself, you need to get them into institutionalized boxes. Since there are such vast numbers of ways to do this, we'll state that you should search for a boxing/printing company to deal with it for you. There are many able ones. You should likewise pursue Amazon's rules on what types of bundling they acknowledge.

Send the Products to Amazon Once you have the boxed products, you need to send them to Amazon. This is orchestrated through the Amazon seller system, enabling you to pick a time when the products ought to receive at the Amazon stockroom. Once more, because of the dimension of variety in the process, it's ideal to state that you ought to pursue the Amazon rules to do this.

Begin Selling This is the hardest part, which is clarified beneath.

Selling the Products

The last step is to get the products sold. This is the hardest as you're on the whole at the impulse of the market (both Amazon's and some other market you may bring to the stage). The trick to getting products purchased from Amazon is viable marketing.

Marketing boils down to a few points - the most remarkable being that you need to have the option to right off the bat draw in consideration of potential purchasers and afterward fabricate request - allowing them the chance to purchase your product as a means to fulfill that request.

While there are numerous ways to do this, you should recall that in case you will do it successfully, you need to have the option to go out and market the product autonomously of whether it will be prevalent on Amazon. The less you need Amazon, the more probable it will be that you'll get people purchasing through the channel.

At long last, we should likewise point out that any business you make must NOT be considered pure profit.

Your profit ONLY come after your different costs have

been accounted for, (for example, the real products themselves, boxes and marketing). It is a new kid on the block misstep to imagine that the money you receive from Amazon will be your "bring home" profit - it's most certainly not.

You need to gather your underlying rule from the gross income and after that choose how to manage any profits made (as referenced - this comes as either paying yourself or returning to better/more products).

Can You Sell Food on Amazon?

Everybody needs to expand to their business; the online marketplace is an incredible way to deal with selling your products. If you are eager to sell your products online on Amazon; here are the couple of things that you ought to need to learn about selling on Amazon.

Step by step instructions to sell food on Amazon

Notwithstanding selling food, numerous small businesses sell their products on Amazon. Amazon has a quickly developing Grocery and Gourmet Food department. Amazon grocery is a decent choice to sell your food products online. Practically all food organizations can exploit from Amazon. It helps the small businesses to advance and expand their image.

It helps you to reach countless consumers and gives you national dispersion right away. One of the upsides of selling on Amazon is that your business can have an advantage of Amazon's showcasing just as specific points of view at a cost less expensive than customary promoting and publicizing. Amazon likewise offers shipping and fulfillment services. Selling food on Amazon FBA has genuinely helped the small businesses to reach the consumers that need your products; however, don't approach them in their area.

There is a next to no hazard working with Amazon; people believe that they need to bring down their puts in a request to sell on Amazon; however, that is not valid. Additionally, people imagine that they need to keep up a specific dimension of stock on Amazon, yet that is not an issue. Amazon is path unique concerning the physical grocery store; there is no compelling reason to stress over filling openings in the racks. Deficiencies and out of stocks alternatives are accessible in the Amazon system.

Selling Food on Amazon FBA

Full type of FBA is "Fulfillment by Amazon." FBA is an arrangement for sellers on Amazon where you can dispatch the majority of your products on Amazon and

Amazon will be responsible for the shipping at whatever point they are sold. Amazon is likewise accountable for taking care of communication services, customer support, and discounts also. Amazon is a helpful marketplace where you can support your deals up to three times than previously. Amazon deducts fees in FBA are more than business satisfied; however, your products will sell quicker than before that you can, in any case, earn better profits. Fee deductions made by FBA are rewarded by the cost of boxes and delivery goods.

Furthermore, consider the incredible time spared by not wrapping them for you and ship 20 to 30 parcels day by day. You can save a great deal of time to perform different assignments, like product research.

Would you be able to sell frozen food on Amazon?

Indeed, you can sell frozen food. This is giving offices to its sellers and buyers to sell frozen food online. You can sell your frozen food items on Amazon, and buyers can buy them effectively. Almost certainly, Amazon is the best online marketplace to sell your frozen products online and earn a more significant number of profits than a customary market.

Selling on Amazon is simple for small businesses; you can sell your products as an expert or as a person. You can likewise enjoy the one month of free membership to enjoy the advantages of selling on Amazon for nothing.

How to Write Amazon Product Listing Descriptions?

Amazon FBA, and by and large selling products on the Amazon stage, has rapidly turned into a goldmine for several merchants - who both got in ahead of schedule and figured out how to develop a crowd of people who needed what they were putting forth.

To do this appropriately, you must probably consider precisely what you're doing in regards to the closeout of products, and how they're showcased.

Aside from engaging photographs, the description is the fundamental way people can pick up an insight into what the product does, how it works - and how it's diverse to other contending ones.

This instructional exercise plans to feature how you're ready to deal with the best Amazon product listing descriptions.

Structure

Amazon product listings hold fast to a similar structure:

- Title
- Images
- Features (Bullet Points)
- Description (incl HTML)

What the vast majority find in the Amazon listing is the top part (Title, Images and Bullet Points) - the "meat" of the listing is the description, which can incorporate fundamental HTML organizing. If you need to make a compelling listing, try honestly, brief and exhaustive.The best, for the most part, have clear, top-notch images, combined with useful and convincing bullet points (which are focused on benefits) and a catchphrase rich title.

The genuine executioner the "copy" used all through the listing. Either in the bullet-points and the full description, having the option to pass on the benefits of the product while guaranteeing the peruser is constrained to purchasing your specific product is a scarce difference.

Because of the idea of this copy, several copywriting specialists have been making genuine cash giving "Amazon Product Listing" copywriting administrations.

The reason is they will help people make more cash by composing progressively clear copy.

The most effective method to Do It Yourself. As mentioned, the above structure is practically what decides if Amazon will acknowledge a product.

The most important thing to do is comprehend what "triggers" buyers to confide in your product. When selling products, it's better to manage emotion than rationale.

Sensibly, you may figure the product can be recorded, and people will pick it, assess it dependent on its features, and make a buy. Emotionally, people pick products by the company they feel will convey an encounter as near their yearnings as could reasonably be expected.

Such examples as making a "convincing" title (which simply needs to list the different features of the product from the point of view of how it very well may be used) and a "description" which showcases how the product can fit into the buyer's life will change over a lot higher than just listing the features of the product. Keep in mind, most of the people are purchasing the product for an ulterior reason featuring how it will push them to this fundamental outcome will make the distinction between buying the product or not.

To this end, the accompanying clarifies how every one of the components of the description work:

Title

The most important thing to guarantee with a product's title is that it's as descriptive as could reasonably be expected.

A few products, (for example, books) don't need excessively descriptive titles. Be that as it may, most the classifications do require the most descriptive title conceivable.

Think about the accompanying examples:

AYL Silicone Cooking Gloves - Heat Resistant Oven Mitt for Grilling and BBQ and Kitchen - Safe Handling of Pots and Pans - Cooking and Baking Non-Slip Potholders - Internal Protective Cotton Layer AYL Silicone Cooking Gloves (Green) - Heat Resistant Oven Mitt + Internal Cotton Layer It's proven that the top title changes over higher.

The reason for this is, in reality, straightforward - people trust its more descriptive nature. In a wash of 100's of similar products, people need quality, worth, and assuming that the company behind the product is going to be genuine. Having a descriptive, comprehensive title as the main one will be a standout amongst the ideal ways to do it.

Images

Images are vital for getting products taken note.

The keys with images are as per the following:

Clearness is *everything* - don't stress over any foundation or whatever - people need to see the quality of the product and anticipate that 4k+ imagery should show it Just show what's required - programming products don't "need" a case yet they'll add to the view of its quality - people mostly need to see screen captures.

Make beyond any doubt the images speak to *exactly* what the buyer is getting - don't use any traps/hacks to make the product look superior to anything that It is - show people the product and adornments which may accompany it.

In case you're not excellent with photos, you'll need to converse with a picture taker. On the other hand, there are organizations on any semblance of Fiverr who'll have the option to set up a decent shot too.

The point is that as long as you have ~5 high images, this ought to be alright.

Features (Bullet Points)

This is the place things begin to get significant. The bullet points are intended to describe the particulars of the product; they're presently generally used to give users data about the product (copy).

Notwithstanding what you compose there, there are a few components to consider:

Wrap features inside benefits - Rather than saying "15cm long", say "3 HANDY SIZES - 5cm, 10cm and 15cm"

Incorporate ALL 5 bullets - may entice use 3 - use the majority of the 5 and discussion about the company and "assurance" for the last one.

Lead with "Promoted" benefits - buyers need to realize what the product is going to for them, and after that why - you do this with "Promoted TITLES - trailed by a clarification of each point."

Don't be reluctant to use a few sentences for every bullet - a few products need the features recorded; if you need an extra edge, include a copy.

Concentrate on the product (not the buyer) - amateurs make the mix-up of driving with buyer-driven benefits (because they read it in some copywriting discussion) - this is awful. People are on Amazon to purchase products, not find out about how an oven glove will make them look more youthful and so forth.

As mentioned, in case you're taking a gander at building up a powerful framework, you need to have the option to support buyers that your company - and by excellence - your products are dependable and high caliber.

The way you do that is to make, however, much use of the accessible substance territory as could reasonably be expected.

Description

At long last, the description is the more significant part of substance beneath every one of the details spread out "over the overlap."

Contingent upon the kind of product, and whether you have another brand or set up company, the "description" region can be several various things.

It's ideal to think of it as like a product listing page on eBay - showcasing precisely what's available to be purchased. Small images, a comparable situation exists (you can use restricted measures of HTML in it).

The most important thing to acknowledge is that you're not confined to simply bullet-points (as you are with the product features) - this not just gives a somewhat more creative opportunity. This implies you need to ensure you're settling on the correct decisions.

Lead with the SINGLE reason why people would purchase YOUR product over a contender's - showcasing/deals 101 yet it's so natural to overlook it. There's always a SINGLE reason why people buy a specific product (it very well may be the quality, structure or how it works)

Lead with a feature, use a little piece of ad spot to describe the product and after that use a few bullet points to describe what the buyer will get - you get ~300 words so don't go overboard

Pick an emotive point - The best product is sold through emotion - use copy that brings out thoughts of how the product will fit into somebody's life.

Use HTML sparingly - intense content is decent, yet not the characterizing variable of your product - don't go overboard with the stylization (it should complement the copy, not characterize it)

Suggested Resources

In case your brand new to the Amazon game, you need to recall that nothing will supplant having a successful product. How you show said a product is additionally critical, as an audit.

To show signs of improvement in sight, there are a few great assets:

Levi Newman on Fiverr (likewise scan for "Embrava" on Amazon for examples of his work)

Split - "The Ultimate Amazon Product Description Template" (VERY great data)

CHAPTER FOUR

How to Boost Sales on Amazon Overview

Despite being a champion amongst the most broadly perceived request we get from clients, it is difficult to reply with a single answer. That is because, shockingly, there's no charm shot, yet instead, a related arrangement of tips, techniques, and procedures that you'll need to give a chance in your amazon dealer focal.

In working with numerous clients, we've watched a range Ideas - a few works and some not - that have incited to the deals. So, we have masterminded a rundown of strategies which can support your arrangements on amazon.com, not every one of you may get full learning as indicated by your inclination of business, notwithstanding, some of them will move your business up.

Product Images

Pictures are essential for driving changes as buyers need to grasp what they are buying. In a perfect world, images ought to be over 1000X1000 pixels with a white foundation, and the whole product must be unmistakable and should take up generally 80% of the space. Images ought to exclude watermarks, fringes, URLs, movement, dealer logos, or some other content.

Product Descriptions and Bullet Points

Various clients are going to your product with the other need, so the shorter you are in your descriptions, the more supportive you are to the clients to choose your product. A lot of data additionally drives your client away from your page so product description ought to be held under 200 words roughly. Also, however, there is no distributed rundown, restricted HTML designing is permitted. These configurations are altogether known to work:

Most classifications will likewise permit up to five bullet points. This ought to be abnormal state subtleties that you need to incorporate, so limit bullet points to features with the broadest intrigue.

Improve your Amazon vendor focal record SEO

Just as dealer rating and value, Amazon additionally takes a gander at catchphrases in the product's title to rank listings. Amazon's catchphrase stuffing choice for a product's title is hugely reminiscent of strategies SEO offices use to send to improve Google rankings in the mid-2000s.

With the product title, you have a character point of confinement of 1000 characters in each line, in which you ought to incorporate whatever number catchphrases as could be allowed to ensure your product is noticeable. Amazon recommends including brand, description, product line, material, shading, size, and amount in this field.

Separate to the product title, Amazon likewise offers you to enter data into a catchphrase field. Significantly, it is inadequate to incorporate any catchphrases that you had officially used in the product title, as Amazon will disregard this. You are permitted five catchphrases or watchword expressions to be entered here, so use them carefully.

Promoting

If you are merely beginning or looking to your product before whatever number eyeballs as could reasonably be expected to attempt Amazon supported products. This empowers your product to be shown underneath query items, in the right-hand section or on detail pages.

Promoting outside of Amazon

Although email interchanges and direct calls have a place with an old way of thinking and that can lead people away from your Amazon Store, this doesn't mean you can't showcase people. You can compose Article and web journals accomplish this objective. You can focus on your applicable class with pertinent substance for nothing using Word Press. There are bunches of destinations which give you a chance to welcome your clients by composing articles for nothing.

Limits

Limits assume an essential job in redirecting deals diagram to an abnormal state and building a bond among vendor and buyers. Day by day arrangements and critical restrictions could arrive you at #1 for your product class. This, in the same way, opens up the likelihood of showing up on the Amazon landing page under the "Hot Deals" and "New and Noteworthy" classifications, which will create large measures of traffic.

Amazon vendor focal: Fulfillment by Amazon (FBA)

Amazon enables vendors to use its coordination's network to store and convey their products. Amazon saves your products in its warehouse, at that point packs and ships them just as giving the after deals care.

Running Your Own Amazon Business from Home

Sometime before the internet, retail was entrenched as a standout amongst the most ambitious ventures to enter. The internet has enabled new business people to dispatch their business without breaking a sweat, yet it can, at present, be hard to find a dependable balance.

Although there are a massive number of retail sites on the web, a couple of notable brands keep on overwhelming, much like conventional high street retail.

By some separation, Amazon is the biggest online retailer of all.

The fundamental truth is that not very many organizations will ever have the option to rival Amazon. So why trouble? The best thing that you can if you like to start an online retail business from home is to engage with the Amazon brand and make it advantageous for you.

Peruse on to gain proficiency with the nuts and bolts of getting ready for action with your very own Amazon business. You'll find out that by regarding Amazon as a partner, not an adversary, you also can start acquiring a significant living from home.

Why Start an Amazon Business?

Seeing how you should sell products in the retail condition means understanding what customers search for when they buy them.

Every customer search for the most high-quality products at the least possible prices. If you can offer something genuinely creative, or enter a current sector with lower rates, you can pull in a lot of interest in your business.

Be that as it may, this interest is just beneficial if it transforms into income. Lamentably, this implies a significant jump of certainty for your guests.

Online security is better than anyone might have expected. Anyway, retail trust is about undeniably more than stolen charge cards. It can take a very long time for potential customers to discover that you offer great products, you bundle them well, you dispatch them on time, and you catch up with excellent customer service.

Amazon is the most significant online retailer since it is a brand that customers trust. In case you're selling on Amazon, they'll trust you as well.

How Does Selling on Amazon Work?

To start with, you have to sign up for a seller account with Amazon. There are two types of account access.

The standard basic Seller Account is free and offered to those retailers that sell under 35 things every month. Products can be recorded in up to 20 different categories, and you will necessarily pay an expense for every product sold. A significant restriction, however, is that you can sell products that are available to be purchased on Amazon.

As your business develops, you might need to move up to a Pro Seller Account. This type of account is charged at £25 every month, except incorporates the ability to create new products, and sell them crosswise over up to 25 distinct categories. For more information on the types of account accessible, visit amazon.co.uk/services.

What Can You Sell on Amazon?

In the same way, with any retail business, the initial phase ineffective Amazon selling is settling on your products. Amazon presently has categories for pretty much anything. For the most part, you have three sorts of products that you can sell on Amazon - which one is right for you?

Products That You Make - If you have a great product

idea or even only the ability for making new things, your outcomes could fill a specialty on Amazon. With next to zero challenge, these kinds of products are potentially worthwhile - however, it's unbelievably hard to be unique!

Products from Wholesalers - The conventional retail business model, you could source products from wholesalers or manufacturers and sell them with an increase in Amazon. However, be careful - having stock transported to your home location, for the most part, means buying high volumes of stock ahead of time! If you intend to utilize this method, consider drop shipping, where inventory is dispatched legitimately from the wholesaler.

Utilized Goods - From used books to DVDs, numerous sellers procure a living from reselling used merchandise. At the point when a customer looks Amazon for a product, they will see your increasingly moderate utilized form.

The best kind of product for you will depend on your gifts, your objectives, and the type of products that you approach as well. It's a great appeal to make a decision - invest less energy considering your first products and additional time working on advancing your Amazon business.

One Amazon seller, Tedric P, did precisely this. He

started by selling computer games and consoles that he would buy from high street retailers that were closing down their stores. Presently, his products spread various categories, and he is procuring 30% more than he was in his all-day work!

Pick Your Preferred Order Fulfillment Method

When you have chosen your products, the time has come to consider how you will get these products to your customers. Never surge straight into selling without getting a clear idea of how the whole procedure will work.

When you start selling on Amazon, you have a scope of alternatives for satisfaction. Everyone has its very own advantages, and your decision will depend on the kind of products you are selling.

To begin with, you can keep your business in house and send out products yourself. This adds to your very own workload; however, at the beginning of your work-from-home business is generally the best method. Another great advantage of keeping dispersion in-house is that you can hold control of your orders, reduce your expenses, and even incorporate limited time materials with your bundles.

On the other hand, you could join forces with Amazon

to have them dispatch orders for your sake. Satisfaction by Amazon, or FBA, is a service given by the company that is designed to reduce your workload and at the same time improve the experience of customers. If you sign up for FBA, you will be solicited to send your stock to Amazon, who will store it for you. At that point, when an order is set, Amazon deal with shipping your products - customers can even consolidate your products with the remainder of their Amazon order, or use services, for example, Amazon Prime for quick transporting.

At long last, you might almost certainly achieve a concurrence with your wholesaler or manufacturer if you have one. Utilizing a procedure called drop shipping, you can focus your consideration on advancing products and conveying excellent customer service. You should tell the wholesaler or manufacturer when an order has been put, and they will deal with sending it for your benefit. A drop shipping understanding is additionally an excellent method to protect courses of action with wholesalers without buying enormous amounts of stock ahead of time.

Step by step instructions to Make Your Amazon Business A Success

Starting your Amazon retail business is simple. Making it effective isn't! Likewise, with any retail adventure, advancement is everything. Amazon incorporates many highlights to enable you to advance your products, yet there is a great deal that you should accomplish for yourself. Here are three hints to kick you off:

1. Consider How You Write Product Listings

A product depiction is a troublesome thing to write. It must pass on valuable information while inducing, alluring, and pulling in your potential customers. As you write, ask yourself what your customers would need to know and how the product can support them. Does it make them look great? Does it spare them time? Write benefits-driven product listings that influence customers to make a move.

2. Support Activity Around Your Listings

Investigate any product accessible on Amazon, and you will see product appraisals and reviews. These are vital assets for your work-from-home business.

Ideally, your products will be so great, and your service so stunning that customers will typically rush to Amazon to leave a message. In any case, don't depend on that - dependably be proactive.

You could email your current customers to request their reviews. You could offer complimentary gifts to build up bloggers inside your sector to urge them to connect to your product and review it. You could even get your loved ones to post reviews themselves. Each review loans validity to your listing is that as it may, all the more significantly, can lead you to the sacred goal of Amazon - The Buy Box.

3. Get in The Buy Box

The positive outcomes from Amazon selling originate from getting yourself into the Buy Box. This is a complex, practically unthinkable undertaking, yet one that you ought to dependably make progress toward.

The Amazon Buy Box is the huge 'Add to Cart' catch that shows up on the right-hand side of each product listing. For the average client, it is the central spot that they will click when they conclude that they are prepared to buy. If you sell a product that Amazon themselves offer, they will dependably stay in the Buy Box. Be that as it may, if you don't, you should work hard to get yourself there.

Amazon utilizes a mind-boggling calculation to choose which organizations are in the Buy Box, and the subtleties of this have never been uncovered. There is just one trap - to be the ideal retailer.

Give great service. Send shipments immediately. Use

Fulfillment by Amazon with the goal that Amazon can be sure that products will be dispatched accurately. Reduce your prices and be the most competitive seller on the site. By doing these things, quite possibly you could find yourself in this worthwhile and seek after position.

The Secret of Online Retail with Amazon

Very regularly, individuals adventure online to find out substantial insider facts about their special work-at-home calling. However, there is just a single thing that you have to do to create a fruitful Amazon retail business: do everything that you would do if you opened a high street store.

I opened this article by saying that high street retail was competitive. The internet is the equivalent, if not progressively competitive. So be observing with your products, be proactive with your advancement, and be unrivaled in your sector. If you can do those things, a fruitful Amazon business is simply an issue of time.

Daughter, Sister, Wife, Mother of three, PR Consultant and Entrepreneur

In the same way as other ladies on most days, I appear to need to juggle every one of my jobs.

Digital Shopping Without Borders

Today, development is happening that will always show signs of changing the connection among retailers and their customers. This new retail model, known as electronic trade, comprises of

- Mobile trade upheld by cell phones and tablets
- Emerging social trade stages that unite publicizing, shopping and selling in an internet-based life condition (s-business)

While the web-based business bit of retail today is significant, and a large development motor, the all-out effect of computerized shopping on the retail enterprise today reaches out to most of the local deals. Around 60 percent of retail transactions in the US are affected by computerized devices here and there. The impact works the two different ways. As indicated by a November 2013 overview of US advanced customers by counseling firm Accenture, 78 percent of respondents announced "web rooming," or exploring on the web before making a beeline for a store to buy. The equivalent Accenture concentrate found that 72 percent of respondents discovered said "showroom" or computerized shopping in the wake of seeing a product in a store." Purchasers, at that point, have combined on the web and disconnected into a solitary shopping knowledge.

Computerized shopping doesn't generally prompt a quick transformation; however, it translates to impact all through the way to purchase. While this may appear ostensible development, some real retailers have officially experienced internet business incomes accounting for 14.3 percent of their total incomes as of the second quarter of 2014. The leading 43 percent internet retailers in the US detailed $24.53 billion in consolidated online business exchanges during the second quarter of 2014, a 19.2 percent expansion over a comparable quarter in 2013.

Indian advanced customers will spend Rs 54,700 crores buying products from different nations, and that is required to ascend by more than 75 percent in 2016, a report by installment firm Pay Pal said. "The Indian web-based business space is encountering an energizing time where advancement is the key. Our exploration uncovers that the coming of innovation is gradually reducing borders structure advanced shopping. Inside the number of computerized customers set to develop exponentially, it will prompt increment in the name of customers who shop from worldwide retailers with online nearness, according to overseeing chief of PayPal India.

The rising patterns demonstrate that youthful buyers have built up a strong preference for shopping on the web. It has additionally been seen that the essential wellspring of traffic for web-based shopping and internet-based life movement are youthful customers in the age gathering of 13 to 25. Thus, the quantity of internet shopping stages has expanded and extended significantly in the course of the most recent couple of years.

According to a report out of about an all-out 10 million online customers in India, around a million online customers in India, generally 3.8 million shops crosswise over borders. The standard cross border spends additionally higher than advanced household shopping spends. Average spend on cross border exchanges by the assessed 3.8 million activities cross border customers was evaluated to be about Rs 1.42 lakh per cross border customers in 2015. A Goldman Sachs report in May 2015, pegged the standard exchange size of about Rs 1,800 for the Indian internet business industry. In the study, 62 percent of those studied just shopped locally, 36 percent shopped locally and crossed the border while 2 percent shop just cross-border. That number would be higher, yet for worries about transportation and custom obligations that would be demanded on the products. Inconvenience returning products that demonstrated inadequately or not as depicted likewise added to fewer individuals buying from remote countries. And 53 percent of the individuals who purchased products in different nations, utilized the location of a family or a companion in another nation.

In 2013, the number of dynamic sellers taking part in Amazon's FBA program rose 65 percent: 73 percent of members who were studied conceded their unit deals on Amazon expanded 20 percent since joining the program.

Alibaba - China's most significant web-based business company that additionally held the biggest first sale of stock in history in 2014 - handled an aggregate of $248 billion in exchanges on its online destinations during 2014, more than those of eBay and Amazon joined. Airplay, Alibaba's online installment stage, handled more than triple the measure of portable installment prepared by PayPal. Alibaba's IPO and business activities blended a great arrangement of interest among financial specialists yet conveyed a valuable couple of subtleties a session on how they plan to work in the United States.

Some portion of their procedure, specialists, accept, is to contact an expected 50 million individuals of Chinese plunge living outside their nation and to give local Chinese people access to the world's best retail marks. These two components, they state, are probably going to grow Alibaba's worldwide impact and have a progressively outstretching influence over the world's land markets.

Advantages of Digital Shopping

Shopping on the web is better for some reasons. You don't need to go out to find what you need; you can evade traffic, think about prices effectively and show signs of improvement limits. Anyway, this accompanies danger of internet security. We are, for the most part, acquainted with phishing sends and the risks of executing on an unbound site and utilizing open PCs or shared wi-fi associations.

Insurance to be taken while doing advanced shopping, individuals ought to be cautious about the accompanying: -

(a) Beware of mischievous limits

You see a 40 percent markdown sign and close you are getting a decent arrangement. Be that as it may, check the present market cost of the product before tapping on the buy online catch. Prices of products, particularly gadgets, fall inside a couple of long stretches of dispatch. Numerous sites, notwithstanding, give limits on the first most extreme retail price. A straightforward arrangement is to think about the cost on a site like http://www.junglee.com. Or then again, look at the cost at your neighborhood store. You may show signs of improvement bargain there, particularly if you go for a trade offer. Likewise, find out about the site's business model. Is it an e-retailer, where the site is the seller, or an exchanging stage, for example, http://www.ebay.in/where the site is only an agent? In the last mentioned, the certification originates from the seller and not the site encouraging the exchange. Likewise, protests should be settled with the seller, not the site that rundowns the product.

(b) Check for Coupons

While sites themselves offer limits and give, you can finish up with a shockingly better arrangement if you pursue specific coupon sites. Barely any sites rundown arrangements and offers crosswise over various sites, product categories, even specific products. Pick a method from here before making the installment to set aside more cash.

(c) Avoid direct bank moves: Pay through authority installment service.

Money down and net banking are the most secure approaches to execute online. However, if these alternatives are not accessible, go for a virtual Mastercard. It is an extra 'card' issued on your essential Visa. Every pertinent detail is available just on the web. It has the legitimacy of a couple of months, and you can set a credit breaking point of your decision. A lot of shopping sites are following the commercial center model; they are a stage for sellers to list the products they are selling. The site itself doesn't stock; it screens the order until it is conveyed to you. A lot of sellers acknowledge installments utilizing Mastercard's, check cards, e-wallets, money down, or direct exchanges to their ledgers. Each shopping site has its very own installment service through which you can pay utilizing cards and wallets. The sites would then be able to follow the order status and help with discounts, if necessary. Carefully maintain a strategic distance from direct bank moves, except if you realize the seller truly well.

(d) Shoddy security and protection approach

Numerous sites expect you to enroll before putting in a request or notwithstanding seeing products. The web trader may request that you enter individual subtleties, for example, name and address. This should go about as a red alarm. Such information can be utilized to send spam sends. Try not to respond to questions that you believe are extra for preparing the order. Additionally, such destinations expect you to consent to specific terms and conditions. Peruse these as you may offer consent to share your subtleties. E-shoppers regularly share your information with partner organizations. A simple method to maintain a strategic distance from security issues is to shop from locales that are individuals from a 'seal of endorsement' program that sets deliberate rules for protection-related practices, for example,

(e) Clear your perusing history day by day

Have you at any point thought about how web-based business destinations show you past pursuits when you visit later? Sites use treats and other innovation, for example, pixel labels and explicit blessing to catch information to track shopping propensities. A portion of these treats are saved money on your framework and are utilized to send commercial flags and mailers, both by the site and outsider destinations with which the information was shared. You can quit this by changing your program settings not to acknowledge treats. Notwithstanding, this implies a poor advanced shopping knowledge typically as parts of the site blocked off. The center way is to clear your perusing history day by day.

(f) Don't neglect to check the reliability of Seller

The appraisals are high parameters to know the reliability of sellers as they depend on client input and how past orders were executed. Any seller with a higher positioning will be a more secure wagered than one which has been hailed for wrong order conveyance or low-quality products. For instance, there might be five sellers on a specific site selling a specific product. Continuously think about their appraisals and go for the one which has a superior record.

(g) All about applications

Cell phone applications are anger among shopping sites. Computerized shopping destinations have applications, and a few arrangements are accessible just through these applications. All the more so different players are additionally pushing applications. Fundamentally, you can shop effectively utilizing your PDA however dependably guarantee that you are running the most recent rendition of the app.

7 Steps to Automate Your Online Business and Increase Sales

Today's entrepreneurs care about being energetic about work and knowing that it has a more significant meaning. As entrepreneurs, we like our job to make some effect and make the world an excellent spot. In the meantime, in any case, we love our work to be effective. We are doing great by doing great. With the most exceedingly awful retreat in decades in our back view-reflect, today's entrepreneurs need to be incredibly inventive and do things effectively. These seven steps to robotize your online business will increase deals and improve your tasks.

Computerization is the way to building an active business with fewer assets. To create great organizations, as a group, and to use innovation, eventually to better the world is a shared objective of today's entrepreneur. And yet, today's entrepreneurs don't have the financial assets accessible to procure a group of workers. So, the more that today's entrepreneur can achieve solo, the better.

Finding the formula to entrepreneur achievement won't be a simple journey or a necessary assignment. You need to work at it. Nonetheless, if you use these seven steps to online business computerization, you can begin finding the achievement and building the future you have always needed.

7 Steps to Building an Automated Online Business:

These are seven steps that you can take on your journey to becoming an independently employed, free, and very useful entrepreneur without breaking the bank.

1. Construct a WordPress Website

The most popular content administration framework accessible today is WordPress. As today's entrepreneur, you will need to choose the correct content administration framework to fabricate your website. WordPress possesses all the necessary qualities. It's free. It is protected, it is adaptable so you can execute these mechanization tips into your website and draw near to reaching your objective of building an automated online business.

Pick an expert WordPress subject that is spotless, quick, and responsive. We suggest StudioPress WordPress Themes. They are fueled by the Genesis Framework, which in layman's terms, implies that the behind-the-scenes stray pieces of your website will be web index inviting, responsive with instant updates and water/air proof security. Don't sit idle with the wrong WordPress subject. Pick a framework that is best in class and one that will refresh with the click of a mouse. Numerous locales are hacked (or don't use WordPress without limit) because they have not been restored and with StudioPress topics, the demonstration of updating your code to the latest innovation takes only a click. You are upgrading to the present form of WordPress and Genesis a snap. Everything is integrated, so you don't need to call your designer. Set aside time and cash.

Initial introductions Count: Your website is just on a par with your plan and your web hosting organization.

2. Construct your Email List

Email marketing is an integral asset that can broaden your compass past your website and create new deals openings. In case you're not building an email list, you're making a gigantic error, so begin immediately with your new business and start building an email list.

Any networking occasion gives phenomenal chances to gather business cards, which would then be able to be physically added to your email list. If you're like most entrepreneurs, there isn't sufficient time in the day to go to each Chamber of Commerce occasion. In this way, to fabricate your email list, you need to computerize. The least demanding and best approach to computerize your email marketing endeavors is with Aweber Email Marketing. I have attempted them all, and I generally returned to Aweber.

To start with, you need to determine who is your target audience. This straightforward exercise will help. To begin with, answer these inquiries:

- What do your optimal endorsers need?
- What's the main issue they have that you trust you can explain?
- What's your strategy for solving that issue?
- What do you want to discuss more than anything?

When you're done, you combine them all. These are the people you are supplying to. This is your target audience.

3. Write Compelling Content

The best method to develop visitors to your website or blog is to write compelling content. Honestly, believe it or not. All the time you spent in English class in secondary school will finally prove to be useful. When you're writing content, you will need to think about the audience you're trying to reach, what's more, get them out. Write evergreen content that helps, informs, and fulfills your target audience.

Evergreen content is timeless content that is as yet important. You could experience your chronicles, or you could likewise use a WordPress module like Revive Old Posts to disentangle the procedure. There is also a fantastic instrument that I use called MeetEdgar that enables you to distribute a post and after that automatically reuse your top posts a few times on a calendar.

The quantity of supporters you have is legitimately identified with...

Your capacity to drive exceedingly targeted traffic to your blog.

Your capacity to change over that traffic into FIERCELY LOYAL supporters.

Your capacity to get your perusers to elevate and allude you to companions.

Presently it's up to you to make a move and assemble your email list with compelling content.

4. Construct your Social Media Profiles

With regards to online individual or business branding, the making of social media profiles is significant. Think of every social media profile you create as a landing page for your image. This landing page is perhaps the first experience that somebody is going to have with your vision, and you will need that initial introduction to be brilliant and make the visitor need to find out about you.

Ten steps you need to pursue to create a fruitful social media profile:

1. Your name - Be sure to enter the name you need to be found under.
2. Your username - Think about what people will look for you, and make beyond any doubt that your username is included in the URL.
3. Your profile pic - Use an expert photo, however less that you don't outline some character. Make sure to stay with a similar picture as your default photograph starting with one network then onto the next. Along

these lines, people effectively remember you over every single social network.

4. Your link - Make beyond any doubt that your link is upfront with the goal that people can find it rapidly and click through to your website.

5. Your profile - Take the preferred position of this to share simply the best about yourself and your image. What's more, dependably - dependably - link to your website or landing page.

6. Your interests - Look at these fields as an extra spot to get some incredible watchword esteem. Find books, documentaries, and profiles of influential people in your industry and include those in these additional fields.

7. Your experience - A modified foundation will enable you to share extra information that may not fit in the areas of your profile.

8. Your security settings - These shift from network to network; however, you will need to make beyond any doubt that the information you might want to be open is visible.

9. Your activity - Once your profile setup is finished, your on-going mission will be to maintain a substantial dimension of

business on your main social networks, which for most will be Twitter, Facebook, and LinkedIn. Computerize this! We like Buffer. It's inexpensive and an excellent method to keep your social media activity at pinnacle performance.

10.   Your advancement - your website!

If you are short on time, focus on the Social Media Big Three:

- Facebook
- Twitter
- LinkedIn.

Don't neglect to interlink your profiles to one another. If you can share various links on a social profile, make beyond any doubt a portion of those is to your main social profiles.

5. Sync your Blog or Website

Include social offer catches onto your page or automatically post on social media at whatever point you distribute another article. Moreover, with Step 2 (above) you will be able to create a blog communicate with Aweber so each time you distribute another blog post to your WordPress website, Aweber will use your job to create dynamic bulletin and deliver your content to everybody on your email list.

Why? Because research shows that the lead nurturing process today takes seven to eight touches. These seven to eight steps that it takes to qualify a lead are essential segments of the lead nurturing process, allowing marketing the chance to instruct and inform prospects as they travel through each phase in the buying journey. These touchpoints are chances to get ready leads for the final stage in the buying journey, the end of essential leadership.

Sync your social media profiles to landing pages that are explicit to your visitor. Our preferred computerization apparatus for change optimization is Thrive Leads Landing Pages. Assemble an automated deals pipe that runs a very optimized.

Sync your website with an opt-in form so your visitors can without much of a stretch buy into your pamphlet:

Aweber has numerous templates that you can use to add an opt-in form to your website.

ThriveLeads has various "triggers." Trigger options can be the following:

- Show on page load
- Show after a specific timeframe.
- Show when the user scrolls to a particular piece of the content.

- Show when the user scrolls to a level of the route down the content.
- Show when the user is going to leave the page (leave intent) - this trigger option does not work on cell phones.
- Show when the form enters the viewport.
- Show when the user clicks a component.
- Shows on click.

Alter which opt-in form shows, when and where with ThriveLeads. You can arrange every one of the ways you need to display automatically on the site into various Lead Groups. Within each Lead Group, you can create and alter different opt-in forms without a moment's delay, set them to show up in multiple places, and set up A/B tests.

We "interface" our ThriveLeads form to Aweber's API with the goal that when a visitor completes the opt-in form, their email address is automatically added to our master email list at Aweber. What's more, from within Aweber, we have a blog communicated setup, so when another blog post is distributed, a smart bulletin is automatically created using their template.

Amazon as a Marketing Tool

I am appreciative that Amazon is there for me to utilize and make money with. There is nothing else like it, take a gander at Barnes and Noble for instance. They are a chain of book stores as well as have an online nearness only like Amazon. They don't have the audience, power, or free devices for authors that Amazon does and in this way are not as effective. In my opinion, you are missing out if you don't utilize all Amazon brings to the table you as an author.

You might be familiar with the Amazon emailing campaign that a few authors have tried and state truly works. I have not pursued this campaign but instead thought it was interesting enough to mention. I got notification from an author that after sending out an email to numerous people, his ranking went up considerably and his book achieved number one status on Amazon.com The email he conveyed begins by saying that he is doing an experiment and needs assistance in becoming an Amazon.com bestseller. It is practically like a chain letter asking the recipient to send the email on to 10 of their friends and family or more if possible and request that they pass it endlessly and on. The email at that point proceeds to explain about the book and thank the peruser.

I am getting reviews on Amazon.

The easiest way to get reviews on Amazon or anyplace else is to request them. At the point when my books wound up available on Amazon. There were a couple of people that composed reviews for them. I needed more. I, for one, kept in touch with every one of my customers that had obtained my books and inquired as to whether they would be interested in writing a review for my book on Amazon. I had a great reaction and tried to send them a written by hand card to say thanks in the mail after they posted their review. This goes far.

We are giving reviews on Amazon.

Another way to get more traffic to your books is to give reviews on Amazon for similar books or your competition. People who take a gander at those books will see your report and may click through to your publication or website. I review each book I read, regardless of the topic. I realize the amount I appreciate getting a decent review; thus, I attempt to do likewise for other people.

Amazon Advantage.

Amazon Advantage is a great way to get your book seen. A few people automatically go to Amazon when they are looking for a book. They may not necessarily search a search engine for a book topic they are interested in to find your website. This is a generally excellent reason to have your book on Amazon. If your site page is on the first page of a noteworthy search engine for your keywords, you might not be so interested in doing this, but instead, I would highly recommend listing your book with the Amazon Advantage program. Another reason to list your book with Amazon is that people trust Amazon, so they are bound to input their credit card information and request your book. They may not know your identity or completely trust you or your website, so having this option will help support sales.

Additionally, Amazon will sell your book at different prices; they offer sales or discounts, yet don't stress; you still get a similar measure of money in any case. So, for a bargain hunter, Amazon is the place they will go to. You can offer signed copies on your website, which is something Amazon does not provide or even packages of your book with other authors' books or special reports.

Another reason people visit Amazon for book buys is that they can combine their buys with other book arranges and get free shipping, your book could be included in that promotion. The best reason to sell through Amazon is that it gives you credibility when your book is on Amazon just like your website. Regardless of whether your website is the first one that comes up for your keywords, you can make a lot more sales through Amazon.

List mania.

List mania is a great way to grandstand a list of books you like and why. You can coordinate with different authors, and both make lists that include every other book to help advance one another. You can have the same number of records as you like under the same number of topics as you like. This additionally gives your perusers a chance to see that you are a genuine individual, much the same as them and have opinions about different books and authors.

Search Inside the Book.

I highly recommend you sign up for Search Inside the Book; this gives somebody who is trying to decide if they should purchase your book a glimpse into what you bring to the table. They may peruse your chapter by chapter list and a specific item they are looking for might hop out at them, causing them to purchase your book. You are just showing a couple of pages, and this can be a great way to get more sales.

Sell yours utilized! Using Amazon Marketplace to make more money.

I utilize this element regularly and sell numerous books this way. You can sell a shiny new book, a no longer available edition, a signed copy or a returned or harmed copy and still make some money.

If you receive any profits back or have any book copies that are not "immaculate" list them on Amazon marketplace at a less expensive cost, I make more money on those sales regardless of whether the book is selling for not precisely an ideal copy on Amazon.

It has been my experience that Amazon offers excellent customer service through email. They fork over the required funds and on time in the meantime, consistently. You can go online to check the status of your record, what several copies they have, what number of have been sold, and how a lot of cash you are making. I have additionally had columnists find me through Amazon and after that interview me for stories, so having a nearness on Amazon is a big in addition to in numerous ways.

CHAPTER FIVE

Amazon Rainforest

Spreading far and wide over the soils of Brazil, Venezuela, Peru, Colombia, Ecuador, Bolivia, Guyana, and Suriname, sheltering an area of 5,500,000 km² (2,123,562 sq. mi) is the world's biggest tropical rain forest with many species of wildlife, and some of them are undiscovered cutting-edge. It was even learned to be cast a ballot in the new seven wonders of Nature in 2009. Not only as a rainforest untouched but since of its variation in flora and fauna in addition to the climate and its vastness, it observes a high spot among most beautiful places found on Earth. Not to overlook; however, this is a living research center, a rich save of Carbon and a storage facility of Oxygen, and it's our top need to ensure it.

It is believed that the name Amazon is said to emerge from a war Francisco de Orellana battled with a tribe of Tapuyas and different tribes from South America. The women of the tribe fought alongside the men, just like the custom among the entire tribe. Orellana got the name Amazonas from the ancient Amazons of Asia and Africa depicted by Herodotus and Diodorus in Greek legends.

Rainforest is more likely than not been formed during the Eocene. It is more likely than not formed following a worldwide reduction of tropical temperatures when the Atlantic Ocean expanded sufficiently to give warm and sodden climate to the Amazon basin. Since its formation it more likely than not been existed how it is for around 55 million years for the most part free of Savannah type biomes. When the climate wound up drier, the Savannah spread broadly.

The extinction of the dinosaurs and the wetter climate may have enabled the tropical rainforest to spread out over the continent. From 65-34 Mya, the rainforest extended as far south as 45°. Climate fluctuations during the last 34 million years have enabled savanna regions to expand into the tropics. During the Oligocene, for instance, the rainforest spanned a moderately narrow band that lay for the most part above latitude 15°N. It expanded again during the Middle Miocene, then withdrawn to a for the most part inland formation at the last glacial maximum. Nonetheless, the rainforest still managed to flourish during these cold periods, allowing for the survival and evolution of a decently wide variety of species.

During the mid-Eocene, it is believed that the drainage basin of the Amazon was part along the middle of the continent by the Purus Arch. Water on the eastern side streamed toward the Atlantic, while toward the west water streamed toward the Pacific over the Amazonas

Basin. As the Andes Mountains rose, in any case, a vast basin was made that enclosed a lake; now known as the Solimões Basin. Within the last 5-10 million years, this accumulating water got through the Purus Arch, joining the easterly stream toward the Atlantic.

There is evidence that there have been significant changes in Amazon rainforest vegetation in the course of the most recent 21,000 years through the Last Glacial Maximum (LGM) and subsequent deglaciation. Analyses of sediment stores from Amazon basin paleolakes and the Amazon Fan indicate that rainfall in the basin during the LGM was lower than for the present, and this was in all likelihood connected with diminished wet tropical vegetation spread in the pool. There is a question, be that as it may, over how significant this reduction was. A few scientists argue that the rainforest was decreased to little, isolated refugia isolated by open forest and grassland and different scientists say that the rainforest remained to a great extent intact however extended less far toward the north, south, and east than is seen today. This has demonstrated hard to determine because the viable limitations of working in the rainforest mean that information sampling is one-sided far from the center of the Amazon basin, and the accessible information reasonably very much bolsters the two explanations.

Given archeological evidence from an excavation at Caverna da Pedra Pintada, human inhabitants previously settled in the Amazon region in any event 11,200 years back. Subsequent development prompted late-prehistoric settlements along the outskirts of the forest by 1250 AD, which induced alterations in the forest spread. Researcher accepts that a population density of 0.2 inhabitants per square kilometer (0.52/sq. mi) is the maximum that can be sustained in the rain forest through hunting. Hence, horticulture is needed to have a more significant population.

Somewhere in the range of 5 to 7 million individuals lived in the Amazon region, isolated between dense seaside settlements, for example, that at Marajó, and inland dwellers. For a long time, it was believed that those inland dwellers were scantily populated hunter-gatherer tribes. Archeologist Betty J. Meggers was a prominent proponent of this thought, as portrayed in her book Amazonia: Man, and Culture in a Counterfeit Paradise. Notwithstanding, recent archeological findings have proposed that the region was quite populated.

One of the main bits of evidence is the existence of the fruitful Terra preta (dark Earth), which is conveyed over large areas in the Amazon forest. It is now generally acknowledged that these soils are a result of indigenous soil management. The development of this soil permitted horticulture and silviculture in the already competitive environment; meaning that large portions of the Amazon rainforest are most likely the result of centuries of human management, instead of naturally occurring as has recently been assumed. In the region of the Xinguanos tribe, remains of a portion of these large settlements in the middle of the Amazon forest were found in 2003 by Michael Heckenberger and associates of the University of Florida. Among those were evidence of streets, scaffolds, and large squares.

As we as a whole know, Amazon forest is amazingly wealthy in flora and fauna. Discussing through its wildlife one may find many assortments of native and indigenous species of frogs, e.g., Giant leaf frog, winged creatures like Scarlet Macaw, and the same number of as 2.5 million of insect species. It is home for 40 000 plant species, 3000 fish, 1,294 feathered creatures, 427 vertebrates, 428 amphibians, and 378 reptiles. Scientists have depicted between 96,660 and 128,843 invertebrate species in Brazil alone.

One square kilometer (247 sections of land) of Amazon rainforest can contain around 90,790 metric tons of living plants. The average plant biomass is estimated at 356 ± 47 tons ha−1. To date, an estimated 438,000 species of plants of economic and social interest have been enrolled in the region with many all the more remaining to be found or listed. The green leaf area of plants and trees in the rainforest differs by about 25% as a result of seasonal changes. Leaves expand during the dry season when sunlight is at a maximum, then undergo abscission in the overcast, wet season. These changes give a balance of Carbon between photosynthesis and respiration. Among the biggest ruthless animals are the Black Caiman, jaguar, cougar, and anaconda. In the stream, electric eels can deliver an electric stun that can stun or slaughter, while piranha is known to chew and injure humans. Different species of poison dart frogs emit lipophilic alkaloid toxins through their tissue. There are likewise numerous parasites and malady vectors. Vampire bats abide in the rainforest and can spread the rabies infection. Jungle fever, Yellow fever, and Dengue fever can likewise be contracted in the Amazon region.

Farmers near the Amazon forest used to develop crops by manipulating the forest area. As the nutrient content in the forest soil is surprisingly low (this is because Amazon forest is an exceptionally dynamic eco framework and its gross essential efficiency is high) farmers continue moving to deforest the area for cultivation. Between 1991 and 2000, the complete area of forest lost in the Amazon ascended from 415,000 to 587,000 square kilometers (160,000 to 227,000 sq. mi), with a large portion of the lost forest becoming a field for steers. 70% of once in the past forested land in the Amazon, and 91% of land deforested since 1970 is utilized for domesticated animals' field. Besides, Brazil is currently the second-biggest worldwide maker of soybeans after the United States. The needs of soy farmers have been utilized to validate many of the controversial transportation projects that are currently developing in the Amazon. The first two parkways effectively opened up the rain forest and prompted increased settlement and deforestation. The mean annual deforestation rate from 2000 to 2005 (22,392 km2 [8,646 sq. mi] every year) was 18% higher than in the past five years (19,018 km2 [7,343 sq. mi] every year). Deforestation has declined significantly in the Brazilian Amazon since 2004.

As a result of deforestation, environmentalists dread the misfortune in decent bio variety just as the arrival of the Carbon which could eventually increase a dangerous atmospheric division. Amazonian evergreen forests account for about 10% of the world's earthly essential efficiency and 10% of the carbon stores in environments of the request of 1.1×1011 metric tons of Carbon. Amazonian forests are estimated to have accumulated 0.62 ± 0.37 tons of Carbon per hectare every year between 1975 and 1996. Some dread that because of emission of greenhouse gases, the forest will be unsustainable and will be lost absolutely by the year 2100 in light of current circumstances.

From 2002 to 2006, the conserved land in the Amazon rainforest has nearly significantly increased, and deforestation rates have dropped up to 60%. Around 1,000,000 square kilometers (250,000,000 sections of land) have been put onto some conservation, which means a current amount of 1,730,000 square kilometers (430,000,000 sections of land).

The basin is drained by the Amazon River, the world's most significant stream as far as to a release, and the second longest waterway in the world after the Nile. The flow is comprised of more than 1,100 tributaries, 17 of which are longer than 1000 miles, and two of which (the Negro and the Madeira) are more prominent, regarding volume, than the Congo (earlier the Zaire) waterway. The waterway framework is the lifeline of the forest, and its history has a significant impact on the development of its rainforests. It spans the outskirts of eight countries, and one abroad domain is the world's biggest waterway basin and the wellspring of one-fifth of all free-flowing crisp water on Earth. Its rain forests are the planet's biggest and most luxuriant, and home to - amazingly - one in ten known species on Earth.

More than 350 indigenous and ethnic gatherings have lived in the Amazon for thousands of years, tapping nature for agribusiness, clothing, and traditional medicines. Today, more than 30 million individuals live in the region. Albeit most live in large urban centers, all residents remain dependent on Amazon's biological system administrations for sustenance, haven, and vocations. For the indigenous population, the Amazon rainforest is vital because it is their home, and their way of life is firmly related to the forest, waterways, and fauna. If you obliterate the woods, you additionally annihilate all the indigenous individuals that are left. A portion of the tribes in the Amazon still have not had contact with outside societies yet. Can we decimate the indigenous lifestyle? The general population has been joyfully living for thousands of years. Humanity will lose their language, artistry, stories, and likewise, their knowledge.

Destruction of the forest had prompted many hazardous conditions not only affecting the wood; however, every inch on the planet. We consider mother earth as one entire unit that is continually working and building, and each living species has an environmental niche in its eco framework. As the world's biggest rain forest that assimilates a large portion of the CO_2 that is discharged to the air and a significant catchment area just as a water recycler, Amazon is our responsibility. Protecting it, preserving it and using it sustainably will flourish each living issue on Earth including humanity. Its uniqueness that stuns the entire world will be generally lost for good. Scientists and botanists and different types of professionals that enter this extraordinary green spread find something new ordinary and imagine that the more significant part of the pills and medication we use are from Amazon. It is a hold of medicinal herbs, and genuinely, it is an endowment of god. Visit it, respect its magnificence, and join hands in raising awareness in saving it for the future world.

Are Amazon and Facebook Your Publishing End All and Be All?

Point of fact, Amazon is the leading retailer of books; however, shouldn't something be said about different retailers who have billions in yearly sells? How are your sells going for you on Barnes and Noble and in the iStore? Are your sells so extraordinary on Amazon that you don't think about other online retailers? You don't think about extending your audience?

Understanding what Amazon has done well beyond different retailers to capture the mind-boggling share of book sells is significant. You need to ponder your business. What are you doing well beyond to capture market share?

eBlast - My experience as a reader and author has shown me that Amazon is the best game around the local area with regards to selling and purchasing books. As a reader, they send me cautions to books I might be interested in that interest me, and I can change my inclinations whenever. As an author, they give compelling free promoting, showcasing my books to people who may need to purchase it.

When you are promoting your title, make sure to request that readers "Like" your product and author pages. As I would like to think, this could really compare to audits because the calculation Amazon uses to send out email impact to readers for books they may be interested being used those "Preferences" and most of the readers I've asked state that surveys factor little to not in the slightest degree if they will purchase a book.

KDP Select - In this program, you give Amazon elite rights to sell your eBook for a quarter of a year. You can't give your eBook away free. In return for restrictiveness, Amazon adds your title to their Prime Library, and when individuals look at your claim, you are paid a specific sum that is resolved quarterly. This program has advantages and disadvantages. There are vast amounts of blog entry out there uncovering authors' encounters so I won't discuss that here.

If you do the KDP Select program, I very recommend you don't use it for your new title. Instead, discharge your claim on ALL of the platforms accessible to you and allow ALL of the readers to purchase your book, at that point once sells moderate, do KDP Select.

I don't recommend you forever keep your titles on KDP Select. For what reason would you keep the majority of your eggs in the Amazon basket? That is not good business. You need to extend your readership to however many platforms as could be expected under the circumstances.

KindleBoards - Amazon has done an excellent occupation of creating a Kindle user community of readers and authors. Think about turning into a piece of the city, without turning into a mobile announcement.

Without breaking a sweat of selling and purchasing on Amazon, I comprehend why numerous authors don't sell their titles on different platforms. I don't concur with them. Distributing is a business. As an independently published author, you are the CEO, CFO, and each other O of your company, and you need to take a gander at more than transient increases. You need to get ready for the long-haul achievement and extension of your company.

A couple of sections prior, I said you shouldn't just use the KDP Select program to sell your titles. How about we look at Amazon's inspiration driving the KDP Select program. Amazon attempts to evaporate the independently publishing market from other eBook retailers so that Amazon will be the main game nearby. Amazon is a business, and along these lines doing what is best for its interest. Is that good for your business as an author? Someone who sells eBooks utilizing Amazon's dissemination? No. Amazon has just begun testing out possibly enabling distributors to get the 70% sovereignty if they have their titles in the KDP Select program in specific markets of the world. The amount more market share do you think Amazon needs to capture in the U.S. before they begin that here? Am I saying you shouldn't use the KDP Select program or Amazon to convey your eBooks? Hell no. I'm starting don't ONLY use Amazon and the KDP Select program. Build your audience on different platforms moreover.

I can hear it now. I have "attempted" to sell on different platforms, yet I get nothing! Without a doubt, Amazon sells the most, however from what I've seen on numerous occasions from authors is them promoting their Amazon product page as opposed to keeping up a website (not Facebook wall) and having ALL of their purchase links for different merchants of their titles so readers can undoubtedly select their print or eReader inclinations in purchasing. I see authors supporting their associations with Amazon customers, yet promoting to different retailers as a wrong idea. Newsflash, your promotions ought to be about your book, not Amazon. Authors give Amazon way more free advertising than Amazon is giving them by sending out the intermittent eBlast.

So, what do you do? Transfer your book to the same number of "real" retailers and conceivable. If you don't have a website, get one. You are in BUSINESS and ought to have an expert website that showcases your work. Make a different page for every one of your titles and guarantee you have the purchase links on it. At that point when you advance your claim, send readers to that page rather than to Amazon.

So, since you've concluded that it's ideal to sell your titles on more than one platform and advance your website for purchasing links as opposed to sending customers to Amazon, how about, we talk web-based life.

Facebook, similar to Amazon, is by a long shot the quickest way to contact a vast audience. Facebook has made networks of authors and readers and has given authors a way to build their very own after! Incredible stuff, huh? I can't disclose to you what number of authors have put the majority of their eggs into the Facebook basket with regards to speaking with their readership. Presently they have thousands of "Companions" who tail them. Who Hoo!

But they appeared to forget that Facebook is a business and going to do what will get Facebook the most cash-flow. I'm not distraught at them. My distributing company is likewise a business, and I do something very similar.

So, we should return to your thousands of followers on Facebook. Suppose you are not one of those authors who "companion" everyone and request that everyone joins your gathering. You are focused on quality rather than amount. Quality being people who might be interested in purchasing your titles. It might have taken you a year or two to grow thousands of quality followers. Think about what happened a couple of months prior. Facebook changed their strategy, so posts from fan pages show on 10% of your followers' walls. If you need it to show on a higher amount of your follower's walls, you need to pay an expense.

Gracious, and how about we do not forget, everyone is getting more followers (even the average individual), yet numerous people, like me, don't look down to the base of their newsfeed to perceive what posts they have missed, so the odds of someone seeing your post have gotten a lot slimmer.

You're not stressed, because as opposed to creating a fan page, you have the standard user page that limits you to 5000 companions, yet it's everything good. You advise people to "Buy in" rather than become a close acquaintance with, and since supporters don't check, you'll never achieve 5000. You'll advance on your wall. HOLD UP! Facebook is beginning to caution authors and erase records of the individuals who top off their walls with promotions. That is the thing that fan pages are for.

Presently what do you do?

Never at any point, ever have all of your investments tied up in one place. Particularly a basket someone else possesses. Similarly, as I said you ought to have purchase links on your website, you ought to likewise have a pick in mailing rundown join on your website.

You ought to build your select in the mailing list with the goal that when you have to achieve your fan base, you can contact them.

Am I saying you should skip Amazon and Facebook or other internet-based life? Not. Be that as it may, you have to keep up as much command over your product and contact with your customer base as you can. Presently get out there and assume control over YOUR own business.

Amazon's Policy Changes - 5 Easy Steps Internet Marketers Can Do to Adapt to It

For those of us who have been in the online business for some time, Amazon.com is no short name. But even the enormous young men can change sometimes.

As of May 1, 2009, Amazon will never again pay their associates any referral expenses for paid search traffic. This spell inconvenience particularly for Internet Marketers who put together their whole web model concerning direct linking to Amazon (I know various them). This would imply that the group of these grievous Marketers better find an elective snappy or they will live on the roads.

Is there a way around this?

I concern direct linking to Amazon - No. Concerning profiting through Amazon's Associate Program - DEFINITELY!

What's more, how are we going? By doing what Amazon needs us to do, setting up a website that advances their products. Indeed, it will require some investment, yet it is unquestionably reachable.

So, here are the ten steps to overcome Amazon's Change in their Associate Policy.

Step 0: Setup arrange - current Amazon's associate, please proceed to step 1-

(This is for amateur Marketers who need to tap onto Millions of buyers and products that Amazon offer and subsidiaries who don't have a website)

Setup 1: Get an Amazon's Associate record. Go to Amazon.com and look over right to the base. You would see "Join Associates" directly over their Privacy Notice. Snap-on it and adhere to their simple yet comprehensive guide to become one of Amazon's associate.

Setup 2: Decide to utilize paid the hosting/free

hosting/a blog as your business model.

There are favorable circumstances and detriment with the three choices above. Complete a little research on every one of them to perceive what suits you the best.

In general, paid hosting will give you the most adaptability. Anyway, it likewise expects you to have a lot of information with the servers and domain setting. It does not fit for an amateur.

There is many paid hosting out there. Here is a couple:

- Paid Hosting Sites
- hostgator.com
- bluehost.com
- dreamhost.com
- gate.com

Free hosting and Setting up a blog are fundamentally the same as. These days it would appear as though a more intelligent plan to begin a blog as people out there are long for new stuff and blogs feed these people.

Free Hosting Sites

1. Geocities.com
2. bravenet.com
3. RapidFireHost.com

4. Blogging Sites
5. blogger.com
6. livejournal.com
7. wordpress.com

Coincidentally, if you are paying attention to this as a business, give close consideration to the domain name of the website or blog that you are getting. It will assume a noteworthy job in molding how your business would resemble later on. For example, you can't hope to profit through Amazon if your domain is giveyoufreestuff.com. This domain is preparing your audience not to purchase from you.

There are two kinds of domain, general and specific. For example, a generic domain would look something like yahoo.com - where the domain name would not uncover any information about what the site is about. A specific domain would look like dictionary.com where you know what the website is about just by taking a gander at the domain name.

When you have gotten your Website setup and you are affirmed by Amazon's associate program, the setup is complete, and it's time to proceed onward formally.

Step 1: Choosing Your Niche

Although it is conceivable to have a nonexclusive website to advance Amazon's products, it might be an insightful decision to pick a class like Digital SLR Camera to target quite a particular audience. The more relevant your website is to them, the higher the capability of the website profiting for you.

There are a few ways to find a niche, and I will show you the most direct one in connection to Amazon.com. It is effortless. Go to amazon.com and search for their blockbuster list. Why the hit list? Since you realize that there are buyers that are paying actual money to get these things.

Wait for a minute or two!

Not every one of the products in the smash hit list is niches that we need to concentrate on. Indeed, they might have a lot of offers now, yet shouldn't something be said about one year not far off? Five years? What about ten years later on where you may very well need to resign? If you need to give Amazon A chance to associate Program be a business for you, you have to figure out how to catch evergreen niches (or if nothing else one that can last you a few years)

"So how would I, it?"

Effortless, experience the success list look at the products. Your goal is to find products that either remains around for quite a while, which is uncommon... rare. One of which may be the Harry Potter series. There may be a spell given on people a role as the people continue purchasing books from the series although there is as of now 400 million duplicates sold around the world.

So, if we can't find a product that can endure forever, what is the following best thing? We would broaden our niche. Utilizing Harry Potter as an Example, rather than doing only the Harry Potter series, we can expand our niche and focus on the slot "Best Science Fiction Books."

Consider it; science fiction would always associate with (evergreen), so regardless of whether there comes a multi-day where people disregard harries, potter, I can, in any case, uncover the Science Fiction "gold mine" in Amazon.

So, after you channel out a niche, it's time to go to step 2

Step 2: Decide on the Direction of Your Website/Blog

When you got your website/to blog up (See step 0 if you have not), you have to settle on how you need your website to develop. (Starting now and into the foreseeable future I will allude your website and blog as just "website.")

There are predominantly three kinds of website that we will utilize: Content website, Comparing/Reviewing website, and a crossbreed of both of them.

Content website is content-rich sites. They would provide a lot of information about a specific product. An ordinary content site ought to have, at any rate, 20 pages if not more. This would give the site more weight and believability. Content sites more often than not have very detail information which would teach the visitors on the products. Some even go similar to discussing the history and the fate of every product.

Whenever progressed nicely, a content website would probably be their very own position in their niche with the end goal that people would come back time and time again to the site to get information that they are searching for

Comparing/Reviewing websites are sites that compare a few related products with the goal that the audience can choose for themselves, which is the offer that they need to take up. Typically, these sites are just a couple of pages long and are direct to the point. They do next to no as far as instructing the visitors to the site and necessarily compare the advantages and shortcoming of the various offers given

Comparing/Reviewing sites work particularly well for niches that have a lot of competition as this would imply that the buyer would either be bewildered about what is happening, or that the buyer needs to research a lot to find the best arrangements.

Half breed website is sites that provide practical information and furthermore an assessment of what is excellent out there. Maybe exceptionally attractive. However, this likewise means more work to be finished.

By the day's end, which direction you need your website to lean towards, indeed relies upon your assets and capacity. If your assets can wait, you should need to think about testing every one of the three types. Who knows, you may get one that fit your way of life and necessities.

Step 3: Getting Relevant and Attractive Content to Your Site

All together for a site to be attractive, the site would need to provide esteems for the visitors. Giving enlightening content and audit administrations are a couple of things that visitors would search for when exploring for a product. So where would we be able to get these content?

If you have some background concerning the niche that you have a bit of leeway as you can make content or even share your very own understanding of the product and niche.

Note: Regardless of how old a product or niche is,

having tributes and surveys of the product is always welcome as various people would have diverse involvement with the product and thus would have distinctive criticism about it. If I am somebody who is researching on the product to purchase, I would love to see; however, many tributes and client experience as could be expected under the circumstances to make a sound judgment.

"What would I be able to do if I am new in this niche?"

If you are stepping into a niche that you have no background in, dread not, the arrangements that I am going to share would be all that could be needed to develop the site.

So, this is your main thing if you have no background of the niche:

1) Google it

Google's calculation is very focused on subsequently any search term that you key into Google search would lead you to information that is exceptionally relevant to your niche. All the relevant information ought to be inside the initial four pages of the search, anything over that would either be of minimal relevant or irrelevant.

A niche that is to board would have information that spreads more than many pages. (You can in this way use Google to check how your niche is getting along.

Multiple pages - too wide/intense competition

Equivalent to 4 pages and beneath - great shot and opportunity.

Under five relevant search result (not pages) - either "gold mine"/no competition/niche too tight/watchword not exact/excessively exact.

2) Wikipedia it

Wikipedia is developing into becoming a "Book of scriptures for Knowledge." On account of its editable nature, the information in Wikipedia isn't dependable in educational examinations and organization. In any case, would we say we are last year understudies that need to present our reports to teachers? All I know is that people need information from Wikipedia and they are keen on them. You can get a massive number of catchphrases and information that you can use for your site when you Wiki it.

3) Forum it

People in the online community come together and create their personality through particular vested parties and forums. Set aside the effort to join a couple of the forums in your niche and you can open up entryways that can lead you to information that you never knew existed. One of the principle favorable circumstances of utilizing the forum is that in all probability, the people in the forums will be your clients sooner or later if you are building a content-driven site for your niche.

4) Read about it

Nobody ever states that you can't go to the library or that you can't purchase any books in your niche, right? Consider it, if Plato and Albert Einstein can take in their insight from books, for what reason wouldn't we be able to do likewise? So, make your trek down to a not too bad library or bookstore and find out about your niche.

Step 4: Integrate your site with Amazon's Associate Program

If you go into the Amazon Associate Area, you will understand that there are tons and massive amounts of instruments that Amazon has to provide for their Associate, and you would need to go through them to perceive what might work for you the best. Mull over the visitors' experience and tolerably embed your partner interfaces in proper spots. Utilizing Search boxes, content connection, standards, a store, a Widget, and so forth are only a portion of the ways that you can coordinate your site with Amazon.

Step 5: Directing Your Direct Linking Traffic to your Website

Presently comes the simple part. Change all your direct linking/paid traffic recently connected to Amazon to the specific pages Associate with the product(s) in your new website.

At this point, you would have accomplished two things:

1. Overcome Amazon's Policy Change of no direct linking to Amazon's pages
2. Build a possibly detached money producing website that is in an evergreen industry

Shutting Note:

For those of you who have discovered this Article helpful, do look at the Resource Box underneath and get in touch with me to find out how to get: Step: 6 - 10 - Skyrocketing your Amazon's riches.

Everything You Need to Know About Selling Your Product on Amazon

Amazon is one of the most trusted online businesses. As leaders in the area of internet retailing, Amazon has the best e-commerce technology and the best traffic to sell your products to a global market. If you're an internet marketing beginner, have a quick read through following features that Amazon offers for product sales.

Amazon Features

To give you a feel for the site let us, first, take a gander at the basic features offered by Amazon. Feel free to visit the website right now - complete a search for any product and see what appears on your screen.

Features to notice:

Results always contain a professional photo or some graphic of the Product.

The price is made visible, and it is combined with an offer, i.e., free shipping. Notice how the amount that is saved off of retail is made visible. This is a systematic advertising strategy - Amazon is telling people that the product is worth and that it's currently selling for less than the amount of its value. Amazon mentions the number of items that are in stock and the estimated time that the product will take to arrive at the customer. Shoppers are more inclined to purchase an issue when they are aware that the Product's quantity is limited. Time expectation is also a functional feature for most customers and sellers.

Amazon makes use of Cross-Selling and Up-Selling. This refers to a concept of selling that is based on product similarity or asking the customer if they would purchase another product which is related with the first one that they bought before when a customer considers one product.

Amazon makes a mention of another product that might also create an interest in the customer.

A 'Look Inside' feature is offered to shoppers who are looking for books. This life-like feature allows the customer to have a closer take a gander at the paper.

Reviews - The 'Editorial Review' section describes the product in great detail. Amazon also allows customers to leave a review for a product bought. These reviews are usually reliable, fair, and act like testimonials about the product. All kinds of feedback can be useful for the seller.

 Added Extras - Amazon includes various other types of cross-selling and interactive devices, i.e., customer discussions, a Listamania feature, Wiki Info, etc. All these extras can be used to create interest around specific products, topics, or genders.

What CAN and CAN'T be sold on Amazon

Amazon permits sellers to place their products in the following categories: Books, Music, DVD, Video/VHS, Automotive, Baby, Camera and Photo, Electronics, Everything Else, Health and Personal Care, Home and Garden, Musical Instruments, Office Products, Software, Sports and Outdoors, Tools and Hardware and Video Games.

Please note that you will need to get a prior authorization to sell in the following categories: Apparel, Beauty, Cell Phones and Accessories, Gourmet, Grocery, Jewelry and Watches, Personal Computers (in Electronics category), Shoes and Accessories and Toys and Games.

The following products cannot be sold on Amazon: Magazines and Newspapers, Adult Toys, Gift Cards, and Gift Certificates, Guns and Ammunition, Photo Processing, Prescription Medication, and Tobacco and Alcohol.

How it all functions:

Registration

For your person, to start selling your product on Amazon, the first thing you need to do is register your account. This is a simple process that requires you to fill out a short online structure to register as an Individual seller. If you think that you will need to process more than 40 orders per month, you should register as a Pro Merchant.

Upload Product Inventory

Amazon has made it simple for you to upload your product inventory. After your registration, you have three options for submitting the information that is related to your Product: Option 1: Use the "Add a Product" feature on Seller Central to create one product at a time. If you are unfamiliar with Seller Central, all you need to know is that it is Web interface used to deal with all aspects of selling on Amazon.com. You can use this tool to add product information, make inventory updates, and later on, handle orders as well as payments.

Option 2: Use the Seller Desktop. This is a free and user-friendly desktop application that you can use to add products in mass or individually to your inventory.

Option 3: If you want to submit any info about many

products at the same time, use the inventory files to create multiple products.

Your Products get Spotted.

By listing your products on Amazon, they reach millions of potential customers all day, every day - Amazon's traffic, presently also becomes your traffic.

Your Product gets Purchased.

Buying a product from Amazon is convenient, yet besides, really simple and quick. Your product is easily purchased at the click of a mouse.

Shipping

Necessarily, you are in charge of shipping your product to its new owner. Amazon will send you a notification about the purchase via email when an order has been placed. All you have to do is, pack and ship your product to the customer (FBM - Fulfillment by Merchant). If you would prefer not to handle this section, you could select the Fulfillment by Amazon option.

Money in Your Pocket

Amazon then makes the payment to you via a direct deposit into your bank account that you add at the moment of your registration. You will also be notified about this payment via email as soon as it has been sent.

While we are on the subject of money, let me give you an outline of Fees involved in becoming a Seller on Amazon...

Two primary 'seller' packages have been made available by Amazon.

If you want to sell just a few products or expect to have less than 40 orders placed per month, you can register an Individual seller account. The main fee involved here is a 'per product sold' fee of $0.99 - this means that you pay $0.99 per Product that you sell.

Then again, if you think that you will be selling considerably more than 40 products per month, you should sign up to be a Pro Merchant. Here you ought to expect to pay a standard monthly subscription fee of $39.99 as well as a minor referral and closing fee when your products sell. These fees are related to your products category.

Remember, for both selling options; there are no individual item listing fees and no credit card processing fees.

If you are new to e-commerce, you may be a bit concerned about the idea of doing financial transactions over the internet. Don't be afraid! However, Amazon has developed a few handy features that may help set your mind at ease.

Fraud Protection

Amazon offers its sellers a world-class payment fraud protection service. They have created a system that is ridden with personalized notifications that tell you precisely what is going on with your orders and payments at any time.

Credit Card Facilities

Naturally, Amazon is licensed to perform secure transactions with most major credit card providers.

A-to-Z Guarantee Program

This program is mainly designed for the safety of the customer however it is essential to be aware of a program of this nature as it has been produced to establish a sense of business confidence between the customer, Amazon and you. The "A-to-Z Guarantee Program" has been fashioned to handle situations where a customer:

1. Never receives a product
2. Receives a product that is different from what was ordered.

The customer is initially encouraged to contact you (the seller) personally if this type of product comes. If you cannot resolve the problem, the customer can then file an 'A-to-Z' claim to Amazon. Amazon then sends you an email, which outlines the customer's demand. You are requested to respond to mailing the necessary information about the order and an outline of the fulfillment process. Amazon then will decide how the claim will be settled - this may result in you having to refund the customer.

So, since you realize how to get yourself started, you need to learn a few tricks of the trade...

It's all about the SALES, so what can you do to make sure that your products sell like crazy?

Tip 1) Keywords

Appropriate keywords are vital to high product sales on the web. Keywords drive potential customers to your product; along these lines, it is essential to attempt to add product-specific keywords to your Amazon product description as well as anywhere else that you may be writing about your product. If you want to get high traffic from search engines, you might need to complete a keyword phrase analysis of your main product. This can be done by using Google's external keyword tool, or WordTracker's free tool. There are other paid programs to choose the right keywords to sell better (Keyword Tool Dominator.com and KeywordTool.io). It is essential that you choose suitable keywords, with the highest rankings.

Tip 2) Write about your products

The more online content available about your product, the better it is for sales. It is essential that you write engaging content that will appeal to your market, and make sure that it contains your product's keywords. The next step is to show this info all over the web. You can make use of the 'Listamania', feature provided by Amazon, and you can also feel free to blog about your product or use social media sites for further product publicity, make friends or start a meeting with people on Facebook who possibly have an interest in the type of product that you are selling.

Tip 3) Online Product Promotion Companies

Feel free to complete a Google research to find a list of top product promotion companies. There are many companies available that will aggressively market your product online - with this type of outside help; you won't have to take on the marketing of your product personally. The main downside about making use of these types of companies is that the majority of their services require you to shell out a high bundle of cash.

Amazon or eBay? Where Should You Be Selling?

Appears that for quite a long while now, I have been perusing of displeased sellers leaving eBay to set up shop on Amazon. To such an extent, that going eBay, and kicking the entryway shut, appears to have turned into the in-thing. There are even ex-eBayers stating "How To" books.

I don't question for a moment that there is a lot of sellers who, as of late, have left eBay. eBay is developing, and change always bothers the individuals who are set up in their ways. Individuals only aversion change that is our inclination.

Moreover, a few of those eBay changes, maybe the majority of the real ones, have been very seller threatening. Therefore, numerous eBay sellers have legitimately left eBay, basically because their business models necessitate that they should.

What is the eBay transformative changes? Indeed, some blame that eBay is attempting to turn out to be increasingly similar to Amazon. Also, it could be said that the appraisal is right. eBay has moved towards turning into a marketplace at the buy of fixed-cost products (like Amazon), instead of being primarily an auction marketplace. Therefore, the little auction seller never again appreciates a similar status as they did in eBay's initial days.

The motivation behind this article is to endeavor to recognize and to comprehend the differences between eBay and Amazon. Also, at last, to address this question - given your business model, would it be a good idea for you to sell on eBay or Amazon?

We will get to their differences in a minute, however first here is a quick response to the above question: if your business model grants, and you can accommodate the working and philosophical differences between selling on eBay and Amazon, at that point sell on both. Your objective isn't to allocate steadfastness to one marketplace or the other, yet to create; however, many fruitful selling channels as could be expected under the circumstances.

Why? Because your lengthy haul budgetary security is best served by multi-channel selling. Which is also called, not putting every one of your eggs into one basket, particularly when you don't claim the basket. Without a doubt, your principle selling channel ought to be neither Amazon nor eBay; however rather, your very own eCommerce site - an excellent promoting place that you possess and control.

Alright, back to eBay and Amazon. Here are the

differences, and this will take some time because the two marketplaces are different from various perspectives.

To start, consider eBay an indoor shopping center. On the ground floor, you will locate the run of the mill autonomously worked stores. In any case, on the mezzanine, there are no stores, just tables loaded with merchandise. In this relationship, the shopping center stores are like the eBay stores, while the balcony speaks to the auction part of eBay. In your store, you claim the merchandise, decide it's publicizing and show, and get backing and advancement from the shopping center proprietor.

Presently, for Amazon. Consider Amazon being progressively similar to a Walmart overly focus. Here, allegorically, you should go after rack space. What's more, your little area is encompassed by your competitors. Besides, even Walmart may decide to start contending with you with their house image. Amazon additionally gives store space, yet it is undetectable to customers.

More or less, here is the operational difference between eBay and Amazon. On eBay, you are the second-party (seller), while eBay works as an outsider (marketplace). On Amazon, the jobs to some degree turn around; presently, Amazon is the second-party (seller and market), while you are an outsider (seller). In either marketplace, the customer is always the first party.

Consequently, in any exchange on Amazon, Amazon's presence is always in the closer view, and at times standing among you and the customer. As one precedent, commonly, a customer may buy your product; however, feel that they are buying from Amazon. Furthermore, there is the likelihood that as Amazon studies your business, they may decide to turn into a competitor.

Though on eBay, eBay is progressively similar to a presence out of sight, guarding against extortion and advancing the marketplace, however never contending with you. At the point when a customer buys from you, the customer realizes that they are managing a business free of eBay.

Here are a couple of the vast differences between selling on eBay and selling on Amazon:

To start with, this requirement. Coming up next are straightforward speculations offered to feature a portion of the more significant differences between selling on eBay and selling on Amazon. There are unreasonably numerous product classifications, expense plans, seller advantages, and different factors to create an exhaustive point-by-point examination of the two marketplaces. Which should serve to caution that when you know about an eBay-to-Amazon example of overcoming adversity, that specific achievement might be transferable to you and your product.

Well, known classifications - Collectibles improve on eBay than Amazon; while books develop on Amazon than eBay. Usually, these are the particular underlying foundations of the two marketplaces.

Seller chain of importance - The seller is the second-party on eBay; at the same time, the seller is an outsider on Amazon. This is an unmistakably extraordinary connection between the seller and the marketplace.

Marketplace listing access - Relatively unhindered on eBay; in any case, confined to UPC coded items and by product category on Amazon.

The board style - While both have decided that must be pursued, eBay would be viewed as loose, contrasted with the severe Amazon condition.

Store access - With a single tick of an effectively recognizable symbol, a customer can be in your eBay store; while on Amazon, there is no such symbol, the route isn't coordinated, and four ticks are required to access a store.

Listing page - On eBay, you can make your own item listing page; while on Amazon, you will share a product page with the majority of your competitors, and that page may not be exact for your product.

Feedback - On eBay, you can expect in any event 40% feedback cooperation; while on Amazon, around 10% is more probable. This is a huge difference because one bad feedback on eBay won't slant your standing, as will one lousy feedback on Amazon.

Search ranking - While the two marketplaces use search ranking to remunerate individual sellers, eBay thinks about seller's exhibition, and the item's all out expense; while Amazon positions by price, and uses a Buy Box. The one seller who possesses the Buy Box appreciates an immense bit of leeway over every single other competitor.

Selling positions - eBay offers fixed-price, auction, and auction, also, to Buy It Now; while Amazon offers just fixed-price.

Primary concern: Diversify your selling channels. Try not to depend solely on eBay or Amazon. Use every one of the channels that suit your style and your product. Try not to pursue the group. Settle on your selling channel choices dependent on your involvement, research, and testing.

If you are pondering about my qualifications, I have

been selling on eBay for quite a while, where I am both a Power Seller and a Top-evaluated seller. I was a Pro Merchant on Amazon for some time, however never again.

CHAPTER SIX

Profitable Products to Sell on Amazon

The catchphrase is profit - moderately easy to "sell" products (sell smartphones or innovation products), yet your profit edges will be terrible.

What the vast majority don't understand is that the money you "gather" from a business is simply part of the story.

"Full" retail buys provide a gross salary. To determine the profit, you need to limit COGS (Cost of Goods Sold) and any additional "authoritative" costs, for example, publicizing, warehousing, and staffing costs.

While the charm of the "computerized" domain has urged millions to raid into its profundities, it isn't remarkable. Despite everything, you need to represent profit (the primary concern) as opposed to by an extensive gross (top line) to keep up your sanity (and viability).

The "online" business world intently reflects its

disconnected counterpart, which implies that in case you're hoping to exploit the plenty of chances created with the likes of Amazon, YouTube, and so on - you'll need to take a gander at how they work... as "markets."

YouTube is a market for diversion, Twitter is a market for consideration, and Amazon is a market at item costs. Understanding this place, you in the advantageous position of having the option to determine an increasingly successful way to provide solutions to participants in said markets.

Supply/Demand... The most important thing to welcome that it's about supply and demand - the cornerstone of a "free market."

Supply/Demand expresses that if there is demand, supply will, without a doubt pursue... Over-supply brings "prices" down. Under-supply brings "prices" up.

The most important thing to consider is how demand is created/affected.

Demand is the cornerstone of whether a "product" will sell, and is the reason the likes of "innovation" products always do well online (because people need to guarantee they're getting the most recent and most prominent segments).

In this way, when thinking about what to "sell" on

Amazon, you're taking a gander at which products have demand and are under-provided. High prices may not show the supply circumstance, however people will by, and large either keep down on "trivial" buy, or request varieties of provided solutions.

The critical thing to consider is that a great many people are centered around "supply" (regularly over-supply, for example, you'd see from products which either have a lot of buyers or a lot of vendors ("smartphones" being a prime model).

By selling a "me-as well" product, you may get deals; however, you'll continuously have no profit. I would say in the "tech" space; gains are insignificant because the volume is so high. Balance this with the likes of furniture where volume is generally low; benefits can be a lot more top.

The point is that the "price" you accomplish on any of the advanced platforms is intensely dependent on the quality and integrity of the solution, as opposed to whether different companies are as of now offering it.

To this end, coming up next are a portion of the more compelling solutions/products to sell through Amazon:

Embellishments for Popular Products

This works particularly well for smartphones, PCs, and video reassures/games. If you find a prevalent product (particularly game), you ought to have the option to source complimentary embellishments for it. iPhone cases were generally excellent for this from between 2013 to 2015.

CHEAP-To-Make Kickstarter Products

Kickstarter (swarm financing platform) is a goldmine for the curious Amazon retailer. In addition to the fact that you have SPECIFIC postings of products which have been financed (and the accurate information to help them). However, you have a diagram for products that a market will need. The absolute best classifications for this are in the "inventive" space - books and tabletop games. Presently, the requirement here is to NOT rip-off the products being referred to - use them as a point of perception of what you could buy/get made to complement the demand they have PROVEN to exist.

Boxed VIRTUAL Products

If you can get STEAM codes cheap, why not pay some money to get them boxed? Shouldn't something be said about if you found a few "guides" doing admirably on ClickBank's marketplace (there are a TON of game guides for the likes of World of Warcraft Gold and so forth on there)? An incredible trick is to find a virtual product that is as of now selling and make a physical duplicate. You CANNOT rip-off the other product. If you don't have anything of your own to include, buy their book and modify it or something. The point is that you need to provide a novel offer to another market - with demand ALREADY demonstrated.

Custom/Unique Products You Have Access To LOCALLY

One of the BIGGEST errors new sellers make with Amazon is only doing precisely equivalent to every other person. They'll even utilize the equivalent "source" in China (using Alibaba obviously). The best people can basically "source" their very own products locally (or maybe from their providers) and after that offer them as identical products on the Amazon platform. For instance, you may know a nearby clothing provider who'll sell you cheap clothes (discount) - you'd almost certainly put them onto Amazon while focusing on fruitful garments that are on the platform as of now.

Notice all offerings above depend on there being not many different vendors in the market (while profiting by existing demand).

While I accept the quality of a product is the most important thing, in case you're attempting to make an infiltration and don't have resources/aptitude to put into R&D, you'll need to get a move on the market may have by and by.

This is best done by playing the "demand arbitrage"

game - giving products that have been demonstrated in different markets, and offering an improved/practically identical form through Amazon.

Elective/Secret Trick... To talk from my very own understanding, the entire supply/demand thing is authentic for "item" products like innovation parts, clothes, sustenance, or conventional therapeutic solutions.

However, there is another way...

In case you're acquainted with Maslow's Hierarchy of Human Needs, the "price" quantifier is essential for the stuff that people *need*, yet don't *want*.

As it were, in case that is no joke "level 1" (mental) or "level 2" (security) of the hierarchy, estimating is going to assume an outstanding job since people can get similar solutions from most vendors (take a gander at Android).

This can be seen in pretty much every market - whereby an organization will provide "low" prices because of the general idea of their solutions. They don't do very different, and hence end up drawing in a flighty group (who are price touchy).

The truth is unique. As opposed to being a captive to the situation, the best work higher up the hierarchy - towards having a place (brands/communities), self-esteem (self-awareness/"huge hazard") and self-realization (heritage).

By doing this, they transcend price (although can't escape it) as a result of the apparent uniqueness of their offering (regularly named "saw esteem" in marketing).

They pull in buyers who *want* to manage them and are glad to pay a reasonable price to take responsibility for a solution whose advantage far exceeds its worldly ("substantial") esteem.

This is the place "premium" and "extravagance" companies originate from.

The mystery is that markets react to solutions. You take your products to market. You don't have any desire to give the market a chance to govern you. The power of your solution determines its demand.

The trick I've found works best is to go out and attempt extensive, active investigations all alone and after that provide the "solutions," you saw as bundled products. This should be possible both virtually and physically (through Amazon) - and what's more, it's dependent on you... implying that there ought to be next to no by way of "rivalry" that can influence how useful the products are.

For instance, say you're keen on playing video games.

You may like World of Tanks. Anybody does posting videos of WoT on YouTube with a catch card, so it's not liable to give you a tremendous edge (despite the fact that it will work great if you post great replays) - the genuine trick will originate from running WoT competitions which you post the outcomes for on your site, YouTube and furthermore through the likes of Twitch.

The part where Amazon plays into this is it will give you the chance to sell the "Insider facts" to fruitful WoT gameplay, just as premium vehicles and physical (boxed) forms of any "system" guides you created.

The key is that people who appreciate don't generally need to buy your stuff - they need to show signs of improvement at the game. In this way, what you're "selling" is a way to do this.

You pull in people by the quality of your replays/competitions, and you're ready to offer different products then accordingly they're prepared to recreate. In like manner with different solutions. Maybe you went on a trip to Tuscany and found some unique clothing pieces, or you took your programming aptitudes and created a custom online application for clients who needed to appreciate the fundamental way in which certain things work. The potential outcomes are boundless.

Get Started Selling on Amazon Marketplace - Rookie Mistakes to Avoid

Mistakes occur. They are a part of life. However, errors are no real way to build your trade-in book business, selling trade-in books, music CDs, and instructional DVDs on the Amazon Marketplace. Here are six 'Rookie Mistakes' I made that you ought to avoid if you need to have a long-term fruitful business selling on Amazon:

Mistake #1:

Thinking the customer required a card to say thanks. My initial idea was to build a relationship with individuals who purchased from me, drive them back to my Amazon Bookstore page, and offer more books to a cheerful customer. Be that as it may, the customer belongs to Amazon, not me. Adding a 'Card to say thanks' is permissible under Amazon's Terms Of Service (TOS).... be that as it may, it doesn't generally enable you to make any money.

Bottom line profits endure. You need to pay the expense of the card, the time it takes you to fill it out, and additional postage you will be charged, as you should pay the letter's first class postage over the USPS Media Mail rate when you put anything inside the package containing your shipped books.

Doing this work is unproductive. The customer is not looking for another spot to shop. They are looking for specific titles to buy. If you have what they are looking for, at that point, they'll be back. The ideal way to have an old customer buy from you again is to source those similar sorts of books, list them at a competitive price in the Amazon Marketplace, and wait.

Mistake #2:

Forgetting that book descriptions are, for the most part, buyers need to go on. The majority of the issues I've had selling trade-in books on Amazon were my very own flaw. At an early stage, I was not careful making beyond any doubt that the book I was listing was free of highlighter markings or scribbles in the margins. This is the thing that most buyers need to know since they can't pick up the book and thumb through it, they rely upon the vendor to precisely and sincerely describe the book for them.

I recollect one time listing such a marked-up book as "Like New" because I was in too big of a hurry to thumb through the inside content pages. The spread looked like new, and the spine was increased. Be that as it may, when the customer received the book and thought that it was marked up, he was incensed.

I immediately discounted the price tag, the original shipping and the return shipping in addition to 10%

premium for taking up the buyer's time having him make a trip back to the Post Office to return the book.

Be that as it may, I figured out how to be additional careful describing my books. I, as a rule, take more time to list books now - sometimes three times as long - as I flip through pages of the book, looking for markings or new edition indicators. What's more, I currently list books I once described "Like New" as "Utilized - Very Good." This change has eliminated any complaints about the condition of the books I've sold over the previous year.

Mistake #3:

Not being careful with labeling packages for shipment. I'm a quite good speller. My handwriting is good. In any case, I do get in a hurry. There always is by all accounts distractions when I'm addressing book packages to take them to the Post Office. I have more than one time put the wrong buyer's address on the wrong container. Fortunately, I've gotten the mistake since I have a quality control program where I coordinate the USPS Delivery Confirmation stickers with the right book.

When I fill out a delivery confirmation structure, I flip it over and write the title and the price the book sold for in white space on the back. This gives me an excellent way to guarantee I'm putting the right book in the correct shipping envelope. Indeed, I've needed to discard quite a couple of pockets this way. However, that is superior to trying to determine books, CDs, and DVDs being sent to the wrong address.

Numbers can get transposed if you're not careful, and zip codes could get mixed up. Take as much time as is needed and twofold check shipping addresses, city names and zip codes before heading off to the Post Office. You'll spare yourself a lot of aggravation later on this way.

Mistake #4:

 Not organizing book inventory effectively. One mistake I hold making descends to my own need to improve. By this, I imply that sourcing, buying and listing the books is easy for me; getting them arranged and organized so I can quickly find them again when the orders come in is not all that easy for me.

It appears I have an innate need to relive the frustration of hunting down books for 20-30 minutes when the orders come in, muttering such things as, "I probably am aware I saw that book in this stack... no, this stack... no, this stack." Books that are too difficult even to consider locating and retrieve quickly will waste your significant time, and that lessens your profits when you could be doing something progressively productive... like listing more books.

The solution: bunch your books by subject, at that point figure out a simple way to organize them that makes sense to you - by the date listed, by writer's last name, alphabetical by title - whatever framework works for you, pick one and stick to it. Also, to store your books, you have to put aside one room in your home with easy access, making beyond any doubt it is dry and not very humid, not very close to windows which let in damaging sunbeams, and a tight lock on the entryway if you have little children or grandchildren packing colored pencils.

Mistake #5:

Spending an excessive amount of money on shipping supplies and postage. My initial shipments went in cost cushioned envelopes I picked up at a neighborhood discount store. I paid excessively and lost a lot of profit in those early days.

Presently, I buy the bigger manilla envelopes, and I reinforce the creases and the corners with clear plastic shipping tape, and I wrap the books in air pocket wrap. The wrap keeps the books cozy and secure in the mail (protecting their condition without adding much weight to the package), the unmistakable shipping tape shields the envelopes from bursting open during transit, and I have never had a complaint with the way the books arrive. Along the way, I am confident I've spared at any rate of 30 percent on shipping supplies.

To the extent postage, initially, I anticipated offering First Class Package rates to deliver the books quicker. Be that as it may, the expense is close to 50 percent higher than Standard Media Mail, and the customers appear to comprehend that they are not paying for expedited shipping. There have been no complaints using Media Mail from the people who have purchased trade-in books from me on Amazon.

Mistake #6:

 Forgetting to utilize vacation settings at the right time. When I travel away, and I can't fulfill orders, I always sign onto my Amazon Seller Account homepage the previous day I leave, click on the Store Settings, and select the vacation settings. This immediately expels my inventory from the Amazon framework, and although I don't make any deals on that day, I can focus on packing and getting prepared for my trip.

When I return, I don't click the 'Active' catch in my record until the airplane has securely contacted down at my home airport.

Once I made the mistake of resuming listings the previous day, I was to return home. However, my flight got deferred because of awful climate and orders came in while I was stuck in the Dallas-Fort Worth Airport. Fortunately, because you have two business days to ship the books, I had some wiggle room, and I had the option to beat the deadline once I did arrive home.

These six mistakes were by all account not the only ones I've made along the way, yet they helped show me how to all the more likely deal with my time and assets, so I could make more money and satisfy more customers. I decided to transform these mistakes into learning opportunities to enable me to build a superior, increasingly profitable trade-in book business. I trust they can allow you to do likewise because the main genuine mistake you can make is in not starting your own part-time trade-in book business to acquire additional income. As ball incredible, Michael Jordan once said: "I can acknowledge failure, everybody fails at something. In any case, I can't acknowledge not trying."

Choosing Products to Sell Online

Gone are the days when consumers used to summary to the grocery store or general store to purchase products, they need either for regular use or on different events. Online shopping has changed the way products are bought and sold as increasingly shopping sites are being propelled every day.

Numerous sellers long for beginning their one of a kind

online store. The opportunity to make a large number of dollars by turning into the following enormous online retailer is charming. The first central issue that worries the sellers is the thing that products to sell online. Which product will win more benefits and expand deals online?

Here is a rundown of probably the most prevalent products to sell online:

1.Books:

A great many books are sold online consistently. The online market is commanded by the world's biggest book store known as Amazon, yet that doesn't imply that you are up to the creek without a paddle if you go facing them. There are such a large number of various specialties of books that can be focused towards multiple gatherings of individuals. For whatever length of time that you find a decent hobby and target it to the correct clients, you can, at present, become fruitful.

2. Computer accessories:

As most of the populace is getting to be computer proficient, the interest in computer equipment and programming is persistently rising. Computer-related merchandise is a standout amongst the most profitable products to sell online these days.

3. Garments and accessories:

The style-conscious age invests hours on the shopping sites scanning for the most fashionable clothes and accessories. There is a wide range of styles and costs purposes of design and gems that you can begin selling online.

4. Blessings, toys, and computer games:

These products sell like hot cakes online during the Christmas season just as usually consistently. A portion of these products as of now have a huge fan base that energetically anticipates for the following adaptation or part.

5. Music and movie DVDs:

Research has demonstrated that an ordinary consumer spends twofold the measure of cash on purchasing music and movie DVDs online than they do at movie theaters or shows. Individuals love to gather their preferred music and movies.

6. Electronics:

The Internet offers better and progressively near surveys for consumers, particularly with regards to electronics and apparatuses. That is significant to a higher degree of motivation to shop online for these sorts of products.

7. Other profitable products

Health products, beauty care products, home, and office supplies, home stylistic layout, blossoms, and even nourishment can be bought and sold online. You can find pretty much anything online at a not too bad cost. So, there are no constraints of products to sell online.

CHAPTER SEVEN

How to Sell on Amazon for Beginners

There's another way that allows you to make money selling on Amazon. I'm going to educate you concerning the main ones in this article.

As a matter of first importance, Amazon Marketplace. The Marketplace offers you an opportunity to sell products (books as well all in all scope of things) on precisely the same page on Amazon's site where Amazon sell the product themselves. So, you get the chance to compete with them head-on and even had the opportunity to compete with them on price. Selling prices are fixed - Marketplace isn't bartering. You can list a large number of items for nothing yet what they call a referral fee is charged on every sale. The Marketplace is for both new and used products.

The Marketplace is appropriate whether you need to make some spare cash part-time, yet additionally, if you need to start a 'proper' private venture. The other primary approach to make money is Amazon Associates. Partners is a subsidiary program.

Step by step instructions to Sell on Amazon Marketplace. It's, to begin with, Amazon Marketplace.

You don't need to register ahead of time. You can open a seller account when you list your first product.If you as of now have a purchaser account on Amazon, you can add your seller account to that.

To register as a seller, you will need a business name, an address, a screen name, a Visa, and a telephone contact number. That is all you need to begin.

Go to the Amazon site, look down the page to 'Make Money with Us' and after that 'Sell on Amazon.' You will, at that point see two options:

Sell a little or sell a lot? Amazon offers two passage points into Marketplace, which they casually tag as 'selling a bit' or 'selling a lot.'

Basically 'a bit' is for infrequent and side interest sellers who expect to sell under 35 items every month. You are likewise confined to the product classes you can sell it. In any case, the favorable position is that it costs virtually nothing to start and no progressing charges are assuming, at first, you don't sell without a doubt.

Selling 'a lot' is for professional sellers who expect to sell more than 35 items per month. You pay a $28.75 monthly fixed fee and a referral fee. You can trade in all the Amazon product classifications.

It isn't always practical to list low price, low volume products as a 'sell a bit' seller. To do that you need to be a 'sell a lot' seller! In any case, I'd prescribe you take the 'selling a bit' course to start with. You can generally upgrade later.

Pick your option; at that point, fill in the online structure.

Pro Merchant Sellers

When you are selling 'a lot' you will probably additionally need to move toward becoming what Amazon call a Pro Merchant Seller. Pro Merchants approach volume selling and bulk listing tools. There is a web interface that enables you to all the more effectively deal with your product descriptions, stock, and requests. You will likewise have the option to export and import data to and from your account.

When you get up and running the selling, a lot/Pro Merchant option will work out a lot cheaper and, importantly, will enable you to work on more tightly edges and make money from sales that the individuals who sell only a little can't.

Amazon Marketplace Selling - how to sell your products

Presently how about we investigate precisely how you put products available to be purchased on Amazon Marketplace. The possibility of Marketplace is that you sell your product on the very same page on which Amazon and some other Marketplace sellers sell it.

Along these lines, first, locate the proportionate new product in the Amazon list. Use the 'Search' apparatus at the top of the Amazon home page. Put in the product type name, and Amazon will naturally take you to the right page to list it.

Next, check cautiously that the product type, brand, and model number or whatever Amazon has found for you is the right one.

When you achieve that page, you'll discover a catch called 'Sell Yours Here.' Click on it, sign in to your seller account, and you would now be able to list your product right away.

Presently this is the extremely tricky thing about Amazon.

Expecting the product as of now exists in the Amazon index, a listing is instant for you to use. You don't need to compose a description or upload a photo. You should state what condition your product is in (for example new or one of a few standard used specifications), indicate the amount you have available to be purchased and fill in the price you require. Additionally, decide what postage options you need to offer. (At this stage you can likewise determine if you are eager to send the product to another country or not.)

If you wish, you can add a further description up to 2,000 characters (not words). This will help you to separate your product or offering from Amazon and different sellers.

At that point, Amazon will give you an outline of your listing to check and furthermore affirm what their fees will be if the item sells. In case you're happy with this click 'Present Your Listing,' and you're off. When you've done this, your item is naturally listed until it sells or for 60 days (uncertainty in case you're a Pro Merchant).

What's an ASIN? ASIN represents Amazon Standard Identification Number. Pretty much every product on their site has its very own ASIN - a remarkable code they use to distinguish it. If you know the ASIN, you can list it straightforwardly utilizing that. (For books, the ASIN is equivalent to the ISBN on the coat.)

Selling on Amazon and Making Money

Amazon is among the most prominent and most mainstream web-based shopping sites. A large number of online customers utilize the site every day to purchase different items. Nearly anything is promptly accessible on the site, and buyers can buy anything, and some genuine models are cell phones, television sets, smartphones some more. Such a significant number of people presently sell their products on Amazon since they appreciate the advantage of achieving bunches of planned clients. Dissimilar to eBay, clients of Amazon are not required to place offers. Therefore, the products have costs listed in addition to an extra shipping expense. The following are valuable tips on the best way to make money selling on Amazon.

The underlying advance you have to take if you wish to make money selling items on Amazon is to create an account. Likewise, you can peruse online aides and directions that make the procedure less complicated. By making your seller account, you are similarly expected to list down the items you might want to sell. You should remember anyway that specific products can't be sold on Amazon. To discover increasingly about the limitations, visit the page that harps on actualities and data. This is significant for people considering how to make money selling on Amazon

Charges are unmistakably shown for sellers during the underlying signup and sellers have the choice of picking between two account types. One is most appropriate for people who expect to sell a lot of items while the other bundle is intended for sellers who plan on selling just a couple of things. Notwithstanding, expenses charged change contingent upon account type chose.

If you are considering how to make money selling on Amazon, you will be happy to discover that the site offers a remarkable open door for people who plan to change this into a business idea. Sellers have expected to take pictures of products they might want to sell after which they can list them on the site. In spite of this, sellers are required to ship their product to Amazon. Endless supply of the methods, Amazon will ship the offered products to shoppers who make purchases subsequently enabling sellers to monitor the stock of their products effortlessly.

There is likewise an option of selling items all alone if you wish to realize how to make money selling on Amazon. In this way, you would need to take pictures of your product and list it in the most reasonable class. Remember to make a thoughtful depiction of your product to make it simpler for buyers to comprehend what they are acquiring. Graphic representations and great pictures decrease occasions where buyers return items. Besides, estimating must be done well because different sellers will likewise value their products intensely.

One more significant point to remember concerning how to make money selling on Amazon quicker is snappy shipping. Items sold ought to ideally be shipped to the buyers inside two days. Likewise, remember to answer quickly to messages from buyers as this will keep them from making purchases from different sellers.

How to Make Money Selling on Amazon - Helpful Tips to Get Started

So, you are interested in learning how to make money selling on Amazon and winning affiliate commissions for your endeavors. Numerous internet marketers are capitalizing on the blast in the ubiquity of the internet and online shopping. Understanding how to make money selling on Amazon can prompt an active internet business. Inside this article, I will provide some supportive tips that can enable you to unite this all.

Knowing how to make money selling on Amazon isn't advanced science. I have helped numerous others with no experience begin, and I am continually getting Thank You calls from them as they achieve new objectives. The most effective method to make money selling on Amazon takes some understanding and information about what to do and when.

It requires a specific skill set to get a crusade ready for action effectively. First off, you have to choose which stage of manufacturing a website to utilize, I like Word Press. Keep in mind, Amazon.com should affirm your site at the time you apply for the affiliate program. I recommend merely getting a useful website ready for action about ANY product you don't need anything, extravagant provide someone of a kind substance. You will escape, and after that, you will almost certainly sell utilizing Amazon.com connections and flags.

As I said before, knowing how to make money selling on Amazon isn't that troublesome, yet it requires you to apply some essential internet marketing principles and techniques. A portion of these would include: looking into keywords, building major websites (accessible presently), learning SEO (site design improvement), webpage advancement, composing promotion duplicate, and numerous others. Fortunately, these things are something anybody can do.

The fruitful internet marketers, the ones who skill to make money selling on Amazon, and with other affiliate systems make them thing in common. Great Training.

Can any anyone explain why affiliates love selling products for Amazon.com?

To name a few.....

- HUGE Product Selection
- Amazon is a confided in source on online shopping (Credibility)
- Hefty Commissions

- Easy to oversee affiliate program
- Helpful affiliate details
- Natural rankings in Google for new products
- And numerous others

Learning how to make money selling on Amazon is an extraordinary begin if you are interested in internet marketing. Amazon is an exceedingly respectable online shopping goal and enables your webpage to pick up the guest's certainty. Building up your skill set is every one of that shields you from gaining incredible commissions from Amazon.com. Anybody with the craving to do this can succeed!

Selling products from Amazon.com is an incredible approach if you are getting into affiliate marketing. When you learn and apply the correct techniques, you will most likely set up ongoing battles freely. The opportunity will introduce itself at each corner. The faster you begin learning is, the quicker you start acquiring!

7 Tips for Selling on Amazon

Selling stock on Amazon is an incredible method to gain some additional money, or even to make a full-time living. If you need to augment your online potential, at that point, these seven hints for Amazon selling will help.

Pick the right seller account.

Before starting to sell on Amazon, it is essential to enlist for the right seller account. You will have two options:

- **Standard account:** All you need to do to start selling is to create a first Amazon account. However, you will be charged a fee for each item that you sell, over the level of the sale that Amazon keeps.
- **Pro-shipper account:** The additional fee per sale is gone, yet for this account, you should pay a month to month fee. This allows you to create a new listing if the goods you need to sell don't as of now exist on Amazon, however.

Consider the account that would be the best for your circumstance, and recollect that it is anything but difficult to switch between them.

Research constantly

You should explore Amazon as you start to choose what to sell on the web. Utilizing apparatuses, for example, the Bestsellers list in the classifications identifying with your specialty market will assist you with knowing where to start. Notwithstanding when you have discovered your first product to sell, however, you should continue to commit some time each week to look into new items, and guaranteeing that your current goods are as yet selling effectively.

Find the right category.

Don't take a stab at listing any old item in any former category; it will be evacuated! Amazon is a simple website to explore, with a very much arranged inventory. Spend some time experiencing it and make beyond any doubt you know precisely where your stock should fit. You don't need to create new product listing pages if the item you intend to sell as of now exists on the website.

Be honest

There is no reason for attempting to imagine that an item is new if it's shabby and self-destructing! Be honest in your portrayals of the state of the things you have available to be purchased and your purchasers will regard it. Continue to wind reality, and you may find your products expelled from the Amazon website.

Be competitive

Evaluating your products is a troublesome ability to ace.

You don't need to be the least expensive seller to make money; with accurate product portrayals and extraordinary customer administration, individuals are regularly arranged to spend a little bit more. In spite of that, you do need to make beyond any doubt, the value that you embed into your listing is competitive. Do some exploration on different websites and see precisely how much your goods sell for on a scope of various locales; this will improve your point of view with regards to filling in that terrifically prominent figure.

Worth customer administration

Feedback probably won't be as crucial on Amazon all things considered on eBay yet that is no reason not to make customer administration your most high need. Make beyond any doubt, you generally react to questions and inquiries rapidly and dispatch your items as quick as could reasonably be expected. These little contacts will make a customer feel increased in value, and in this way bound to purchase from you again should they require a comparable product later on.

Get Amazon

Amazon is your companion. The more money you make, the more money it makes on fees and, like this, the assistance framework is excellent. Don't be reluctant to pose inquiries of the Amazon helpdesk and the seller network; they could set your psyche calm about an issue, or offer counsel to get your web-based selling business off the ground in no time by any stretch of the imagination.

ANOTHER TIP

Top 10 Amazon Selling Tips You Must Know:

Most significant with selling on Amazon is to follow every one of the principles fastidiously. Peruse Amazons administers and learn them and follow them. You would not have any desire to spend countless hours setting up a gigantic rundown of products available to be purchased just to be prohibited.

You should have incredible pictures that demonstrate the product so that the customer is in a store taking a gander at the product face to face. I recommend utilizing an astounding camera or re-appropriating to an expert relying upon your product.

Addition Visibility and more sales by turning into a Featured Merchant! The importance of turning into a featured merchant can be "sell or don't sell." To turn into a featured merchant isn't known however from my experience it takes, at any rate, a month and you should have extraordinary criticism, on time conveyances, responding to customer inquiries in under 24 hours and selling a decent measure of items. Additionally, by being a Featured Merchant, you currently get the opportunity to win the Infamous "Buy Box"! This carries me to my next tip...

Win that Buy Box and I promise you will build sales! If you have a ton of rivalry with your products, it very well may be hard to win the buy box. To win the buy box, you should be a featured merchant. You should have exceedingly high input; however, above all else, you should have the least cost for the product. These three measurements are altogether considered to win the buy box however value bests all. An expected 70% of sales are made through the buy box so you perceive how completely fundamental it very well may be to win, win, and continue winning that buy box!

Don't disregard the importance of Keywords, Content, and Headlines! Utilize the whole Product Description space and fill it with Essential Keywords and stay away from marks, tops, and accentuation as a buyer will, in all likelihood, not utilize these while looking. Be exact when depicting your item and give enough content that the buyer ultimately sees each part of your item. Make sure not to try too hard. When I create a posting, I adopt the thought process of a customer and create dependent on that - what might I want to see, know, scan for and so on...

If you need to prevail on Amazon, you should have the mindset that the customer is in every case, right. Some of the time it is smarter to assume a misfortune than contend with a customer when you realize you are on the right track to evade terrible input - as awful criticism can be the kiss of death in the general long-haul sales picture. Do everything without exception to make beyond any doubt your customer is always 100% fulfilled, and you can't turn out badly.

Fill out those hunt terms the correct way! There is no compelling reason to utilize similar words that are in your product title, your image or product name as it will be of no utilization. Use keywords - terms that are like your product that a customer may use to discover your product.

Make beyond any doubt to utilize Fulfillment by Amazon when required because it might spare you time, vitality and money! Amazon's Fulfillment Prices Gradually continue rising. It might be the best thing you at any point chose to use. Figure out the majority of your net revenue differenced utilizing their FBA mini-computer or utilize an exceed expectations spreadsheet and figure it out and first check whether it is a financial expert. Second, the advantages are what make it so assuaging to sellers. Amazon will bundle, transport, and speak with the buyer. If any issues emerge or an item is harmed or lost, Amazon will take care of the expense. If a customer leaves terrible criticism under any conditions, Amazon will consequently evacuate it. So, remember the advantages of FBA and exploit an incredible method to work together.

Make sure to create Holiday Promotions and oversee stock because the Holidays are dependably the most smoking days/months for sales. For instance, during Christmas create a Xmas Holiday advancement, for example, buy 5 get 10% off. This won't just impact buyers to buy all the more yet additionally create higher permeability with buyers. Deal with your stock and conjecture, so you don't come up short on product during those hot selling days/months.

To wrap things up to make utilization of the considerable number of sales/selling reports, Amazon brings to the table. Monitor your selling patterns; see what items are selling more than others. This will give you the chance to cross advance, make changes to low selling items, and have a superior handle of your entire task. Utilize the reports for determining and for observing how well your advancements are getting along.

Selling Your Product with Fulfillment by Amazon

If you have a product you are selling that you might want to have the option to ship to people around the nation who might want to order it, a secure method to get your product set up to be shipped is through Fulfillment by Amazon or FBA. People can order your product from its Amazon listing on the web, and Amazon will process and ship orders for you.

Why Use Fulfillment by Amazon?

Selling your product with Fulfillment by Amazon is a lot simpler than shipping it yourself, for various valid justifications. Amazon will as of now have the product in one of their fulfillments focuses, which means you don't need to go to the mail station and hold up in line to mail packages to people each time someone orders from you. Amazon processes millions of orders every day, so preparing and shipping is exceptionally easy for them.

You don't need to stress over people coming to you with product issues on the off chance that you ship your product with Amazon because Amazon handles all customer administration and will assume liability for shipping issues. They will acknowledge returns and send out another product whenever mentioned.

People ought to be content with their shipping knowledge because they will get free shipping on orders over $35.00. Amazon Prime individuals get free two-day shipping. You can rest guaranteed that your customers are in the best hands when their orders are satisfied through Amazon, who will ensure that they get their product in a timely way and excellent condition.

The best part is that utilizing Fulfillment by Amazon will build your deals because Amazon is so easy to use, and it is so easy for customers to share product listings.

The most effective method to Get Started

Beginning with Fulfillment by Amazon is easy since you can deal with your stock on the web. First you send your product to Amazon, and afterward, you transfer your listings to Seller Central. Your products are recorded in your Amazon account, and you can change over them to an FBA listing.

Pick Amazon's limited shipping or assign your transporter so customers can order your product. Customers will order your product, and Amazon will ship it to them, giving the following data.

CONCLUSION

From its humble roots in 1994, Amazon has developed from a little online retailer to end up one of the world's biggest online stores with various people, organizations, and organizations utilizing its stage to sell their products.

A few sellers don't have the foggiest idea about the best and effective ways on the most proficient method to make money selling on Amazon. The absolute most ideal approaches to sell your products on Amazon and become a first-class seller are examined beneath.

Ensure You Have Enough Products

Although it is essential to have a couple of products when you begin selling on Amazon, it is crucial to have enough products to provide food for interest if individuals like your products and you start getting more requests. This ensures return customers and the individuals who have been alluded don't search for elective sellers

Your Products Should Be Affordable with Flexible Pricing

The ideal path on the best way to make money selling

on Amazon is by selling your products at reasonable rates. Check your rival's prices and alter as needs be. Although this probably won't get you a tremendous overall revenue at first, it is the ideal approach to get and hold more customers.

What's more, you ought to be adaptable in valuing. If you are the primary seller of a given item and there is expanded interest, you can marginally push the prices up to build productivity.

Use Amazon Marketing Tools and Amazon Seller Central

Another route on the most proficient method to make money selling on Amazon is by using existing Amazon showcasing instruments including Tags, Listmania, and Likes, which will enable your products to get more excellent permeability. Moreover, Amazon seller central gives usual reports that can allow you to break down your sells, know potential customers, and discover the effectiveness of your showcasing and advancements.

Become an Amazon Featured Merchant

Being a featured merchant on Amazon won't just get your products saw, however, will likewise make you trustworthy and trusted among potential customers?

Although Amazon does not say how sellers become featured merchant, you can without much of a stretch get to that rundown by having great deals, next to zero client objections and incredible client surveys.

You ought to likewise ensure that you cling to all Amazon selling principles, guidelines, and approaches to abstain from getting restricted.

See all costs and fees.

The best and effective path on the most proficient method to make money selling on Amazon is by seeing all related fees and costs. If you are a seller who purchases products, at that point sells them on Amazon, your selling cost must almost certainly oblige every one of your expenses and Amazon fees. Amazon charges fees for selling and referrals.

You can decrease your delivery costs by utilizing FBA (Fulfillment by Amazon) where you send your products to them, and they handle bundling and transporting to customers.